How To N

BREAK THESE RULES

Chananya Weissman

How To Not Get Married

BREAK THESE RULES AND
YOU HAVE A CHANCE

Set in ITC Legacy by Raphaël Freeman, Renana Typesetting
Cover design: Avi Katz

ISBN: 978-154-507-125-0

Contents

SURVIVAL GUIDE FOR SINGLES

HOW TO NOT GET MARRIED

Introduction

I'm writing this book because of a glaring need. There are countless books promising to help readers attract members of the opposite sex, find the right person (whatever that means), achieve a serious relationship, and get married. Many of these books even make outlandish guarantees about a "proven system" that is certain to bring success. It is only slightly less preposterous than advertisements for deodorant and fragrances that would have you believe that any schnook who uses their product will become irresistible – even without a proven system!

Naturally, I am highly skeptical of these books. They are generally filled with common-sense notions about appearance, presentation, and etiquette. All well and good, but nothing revolutionary there, and certainly not a formula for one who is already bequeathed with common sense to improve his stagnant fortunes. Some books will present tips on how to manipulate the opposite sex, which is questionable both morally and practically if one's goal is really to have a successful, truthful relationship.

Other books will come from a more religious or spiritual angle, promising to help readers find and marry their soul mate. These books are highly misleading. There is no formula for finding a soul mate. None whatsoever. The authors cannot explain why some people are fortunate to find that person in a timely fashion and with relative ease, while others struggle mightily for years and years, and may never find that person at all.

This is a fundamental issue, especially if the book comes from a theological perspective, yet few people will even acknowledge this basic conundrum, let alone attempt to deal with it. The most they will do is confess that ultimately it is in the hands of God, then present readers with the usual common-sense dating tips and suggestions for how to manipulate God through questionable rituals. This is less morally problematic than attempting to manipulate the opposite sex – after all, you can't fool God – but the practical benefits of this remain dubious, despite the insistence of the authors that *their* system will get you married. How do they know? They just do.

To make matters worse, for all the advice given to singles, dubious or otherwise, on how to get married, there is not a single book out there advising them how to *not* get married. I know what you are thinking: singles don't need any help not getting married, and if they want to be absolutely sure about it they should avoid all the proven systems.

Nothing could be further from the truth! Singles need a great deal of help remaining single in marriage-minded communities while maintaining their respectability and desirability. Obviously one who acts like a lunatic on dates will have no trouble not getting married (though, to our consternation, a great many loons manage to get married, sometimes multiple times). If one engages in behaviors that are completely unacceptable in all known societies – say, vomiting on one's date repeatedly to demonstrate the first time was no mere misfortune – remaining single is almost entirely assured. This book is not for such people. This book is for people who want others to believe that they really do want to get married, and in fact that anyone would be lucky to marry them, while insuring that they will be able to remain blissfully single as long as they wish.

This book will help you avoid falling in love, prevent others from falling in love with you, and insure that no serious relationship will emerge from even the most promising dates – all while sparing you the blame and flak singles inevitably receive when they reach a certain age without having wed. I will provide the best and most successful strategies for not getting married while convincing family, friends, matchmakers, and even yourself that there is nothing you want more. Most long-time singles employ at least some of these strategies already, perhaps without even realizing it. This handbook will articulate these strategies and explain them, allowing readers to mix and match what will work best in various situations. No longer will remaining single be a haphazard pursuit, fraught with pressure and criticism that could lead to embarrassment or marriage.

Follow these rules and you will not get married.

Break them and you have a chance.

Rule #1

Just say no

Among the many ways singles can be classified is by distinguishing between regular singles and "older" singles. There is a lot to say on this distinction, and eventually I will get around to saying it, but for now we will focus on how it relates to not getting married.

Older singles are sometimes asked why they are still single. (Regular singles never face this question; hence, being asked this question for the first time is a rite of passage, an indication that one has entered this nebulous, unfortunate fraternity.) This question may be couched in the form of a compliment:

"Why are you still single? You seem like such a great guy. I'm surprised no one snapped you up yet." On rare occasions this compliment may even be sincere. The vast majority of the time, however, this question stems from a suspicion, a near certainty, in fact, that something must be wrong with the person to be quite so old and still single.

Are you afraid of commitment?

Do you turn people off?

Are you too picky?

Are you crazy?

Are you gay?

The questioner wants nothing more than to interrogate the single with these questions and more, to probe the depths of his psyche, to determine his problem and make sure he knows what it is too, but this is generally considered impolite. Simply asking why he is single, then challenging his response and leading into the probe a bit more gradually is socially acceptable.

There may in fact be a variety of reasons why any particular person is still single past a certain age. But there is only one reason that is always true, for all singles, of all ages, in all societies.

Every time he dated someone, either he or the other person said no.

If you boil it all down to basics, that is really all that separates married people from singles. All married people were in a dating scenario in which both parties said yes all the way through. Singles have always had a no somewhere along the way.

The cynics out there will scoff at this explanation, claiming it is entirely simplistic. I in turn shall scoff at the cynics, for beneath this simplicity is a profound observation.

Being that one can only get married if he and the other person say yes all the way through, a foolproof way to remain single is to say no or induce the other person to say no. The trick is doing this in such a way that one maintains his self-respect and the respect of others, convincing everyone that he is a great catch who truly wants to get married, but has simply been unfortunate in his search. This is quite a balancing act, for if one says no too often he is likely to be branded as too picky or not serious about getting married, but if one is rejected too often, he will be considered a defective product.

To make matters even more complicated, the whole process of saying no or inducing no can be uncomfortable, even messy. There will almost always be frustration or negative feelings, and sometimes a no can cause an extreme emotional reaction. True artists have mastered the bloodless kill, but even they leave carnage at times.

Inexperienced singles (those new to dating) are far more likely to be depressed when rejected and create a mess when they reject others. They will typically fumble with vague reasons that cast aspersions on their internal makeup. You can only get away with obviously questionable judgment for so long.

Fortunately, the whole process of "no" becomes much easier before too long. Saying no will become second-nature before you know it. You will be able to approach introductions, dates, and social events with a near-total expectation of failure.

The realization of this failure will be perversely satisfying, providing endless material for laughter, commiseration with fellow singles, denigration of half the world's population, psychoanalysis of oneself and others, mean-spirited gossip, and even books or videos. All these rewards cannot possibly compete with saying yes to someone who seems to have marginal potential, with taking a deeper look at someone who can easily be written off, to looking at someone's good qualities and trying to make it work. After all, trying to make it work takes work. Who wants to work?

Most people expect singles to become increasingly open and accepting as time goes on and their prospects begin to dwindle, but just the opposite tends to occur. Singles will develop layers of shields and scar tissue to prevent them from "being hurt" or "wasting time", and will be quick on the trigger finger to reject anyone who doesn't pass an ever-growing list of tests built from years of experience. After years of saying no and hearing no, this will be the default response and expectation. Saying no will become extremely easy, because that is the common denominator between ALL their previous dating experiences. Stopping the carousel and actually saying yes will become almost impossible.

So cheer up! It is unlikely you live in a society which forces people to marry, so if you can make it through the initial growing pains, your odds of remaining single by mastering "no" are quite good.

If there is anything at all about the other person that you don't like, or that makes you feel even slightly concerned, nip the problem in the bud! Even if the person is amazing, but you dated more amazing people and rejected them, don't settle now! Don't let a potential relationship turn into an actual relationship, and don't work to overcome even the slightest sign of incompatibility.

Just say no!

Rule #2

Grow your nuclear family

Unfortunately it's not as simple as just saying no. It has to come with a passable explanation, one that reassures the listener that you are entirely reasonable and truly wish to get married.

This is not always easy. You will occasionally meet someone who has many fine qualities, shares important things in common with you, treats you well, has no serious objective flaws, and actually wants to pursue a serious relationship with you. This is a terrible problem! You need to get rid of this person, and you need to do it relatively early. The longer you wait, the stronger your reason needs to be, and this person is not likely to give you a strong reason.

One of the cleanest ways to rid yourself of this potential spouse is to explain that you feel toward him or her as a brother or a sister. Everyone will pretend to understand you. After all, despite all the sacred notions of relationships and society in general that have been eroded by liberal, enlightened, open-minded, progressive, free thinking activists who make up right and wrong as they go along, incest is still almost universally revolted. It is one of the few types of relationships one can still openly scorn without being pilloried as an intolerant religious nut who needs to get over his phobias and learn to accept the oppressed minorities around him and their righteous defenders who now run the show.

Who knows when this domino will fall as well? Use it to your advantage while you still can.

Categorizing someone as a brother or sister absolves you

of any expectation to pursue a romantic relationship with the person without denigrating them in any way. After all, you like them greatly, perhaps even love them, but in a different way. Continuing to date them would simply be wrong.

What makes someone you dated a pseudo-sibling instead of a potential spouse? That is very hard to say, but it's unlikely you'll ever be called on it. Just don't overdo it; there are only so many brothers and sisters a person can reasonably have. Use this breakup line with prudence, but definitely use it. It works like a charm.

Rule #3

Get busy

Nowadays everyone is busy. Despite every incredible technological advancement that saves us time, somehow we never have enough of it. Not even close. In the olden days we had to think hard to figure out how to kill time. Now we have weapons of mass destruction. No matter how much time we manage to save, we will always have more ways to kill it than saved time remaining to be killed.

This might sound bad, like most of the world has become a bunch of narcissistic empty shells. Maybe it is bad. Post it on your Facebook page to your hordes of virtual friends, tweet it to the masses of twits who follow your every musing, and kill lots of time perusing the usual array of witty, antagonistic, occasionally introspective, and utterly bizarre responses to your missive. Then respond to the responders, let them do the same, and repeat until everyone is bored and ready to direct their artificial outrage elsewhere.

The important thing here is that this will keep you impressively busy. The world is filled with people who are not working much, if at all, who are doing nothing particularly noteworthy with their lives, and who can demonstrate less potential for personal growth than a potted plant, yet who consider themselves completely overwhelmed with things to do – all of them vitally important.

No one will admit that they have a lot of time on their hands and not enough to do with it, or that they aren't really efficient and productive with the time they have. No one.

Dating, courtship, and marriage demand a great deal of time. This makes it easy to steer clear of marriage for long stretches by claiming you are simply too busy right now to deal with it. You have a test coming up, you're looking for a job, you just started a new job, you're busy with an important project, you're working hard for a promotion, you're going on a vacation after a job well done, you're taking a break from things after you just got fired from a job, you're looking for a new job. This alone can tide you over until retirement.

Of course, you do have to go on dates occasionally just to keep up the pretense that you're serious about getting married. But the more you date, the more likely it is that you will slip up and get married. As with everything, it's important to find the right balance. Date enough to keep your positive image and remain in the social swing of things, but don't make it a priority.

The truth is that we always find time and make time for the things that are important to us. We will promptly respond to someone we care about or need for something, but if it's someone who needs us we will be too busy - even though it takes exactly the same amount of time.

All those extra hours you spend on things with no enduring value could theoretically be invested in dating and courtship. But if you seem extremely busy and still date occasionally, no one will dare challenge you on how you are prioritizing and spending your time. You're busy! You're important! You're busy with important things!

It's not your fault you're single. You're just waiting for someone who is worth your time.

Rule #4

Take a break

Dating can be grueling and emotionally taxing, especially for those who really do want to get married, or at least convince themselves that they do. Because of this, every so often – at least once or twice a year – you can get away with taking a break from dating.

The beauty of taking a break is that it is a complete moratorium on dating, with no preconditions or exceptions. A single who has not dated someone remotely compatible for years can go on a break, and even if they have the opportunity to date a true needle in the haystack, all they need to say is that they are taking a break from dating, and no one will second-guess them. The possibility that they are forfeiting a golden opportunity for a lifetime of happiness will be disregarded in favor of replenishing one's emotional energy for an indefinite period of time.

Mind you, emotional energy is important, just like all other forms of energy. But if someone were unemployed and bummed out by a fruitless search for work, then suddenly had an opportunity for a dream job – or even a decent one – would we accept his saying that he couldn't handle another potentially disappointing interview process for a few weeks or months? Of course not. We would tell him to get over it, pull himself together, and go get that job.

A fruitless search for a spouse can take a greater emotional toll, of course. The search is much more personal, the stakes are higher, and it is far more difficult to be sure of one's decisions.

This is why singles are given much more leeway in taking breaks and closing off dating opportunities during that time.

Nevertheless, here too sometimes a person needs to pull himself together, get over his past disappointments, and go give happiness a chance – even if the timing is not entirely convenient from an emotional standpoint. We can't simply assume that the right opportunity won't come along when we're emotionally bummed out.

That is, of course, if they really want to get married and are willing to do what it takes.

Fortunately, few people will expect such a herculean effort from you. Combine being a little busy with a little burned out, and you can safely get away with taking a break for a couple of months, no questions asked. If you are willing to invest in seeing someone for a while before breaking up, you can then take a break for even longer.

Don't go on breaks too often or for too long, since you might get a reputation for being emotionally fragile. But if you don't take advantage of this once in a while, you are really missing out on staying blissfully single while everyone will think you're taking that break only because you really do want to get married so badly that it hurts too much to try.

What could be sweeter than that?

Rule #5
Just be friends

Earlier we discussed the strategy of telling eligible dates that you view them as a brother or sister. Unfortunately, one can only have so many brothers and sisters. But fear not! There is no limit to the number of friends you can have, even outside of social media.

This can help you stay single in two ways. The first, of course, is to dump an otherwise promising date because you view him more as a friend. By this you mean that you really enjoy his company, feel you can relate to him, and you are even comfortable talking about personal things with him – but under no circumstances do you want a romantic relationship with the person.

Why wouldn't you want a romantic relationship with such a person? Obviously, because he's just a friend. Makes perfect sense, and you're unlikely to be challenged on this one. If you are, just say that you don't feel sparks or chemistry (more on that later).

But there is an even better way that expanding your circle of friends can help you stay single. If someone you are friends with suggests taking the relationship to the next level, or someone tries fixing the two of you up, you can say that you don't think it's a good idea for you to date, lest you jeopardize the friendship. After all, the probability of it not working out is always high, and then it might become awkward or messy. Why risk a good friendship like that?

There is a delightful inconsistency here. Apparently, if you break up with someone you weren't friends with previously, you can "just be friends". But if you try a romantic relationship with a pre-existing friend and it doesn't work out, you can't go back to just being friends anymore. That friendship is spoiled forever. Why is that so? How does this work?

Who knows? Who cares?

You have a good way of terminating a relationship on the one hand and avoiding one on the other hand. It sounds reasonable, respectful, and sensitive on the surface. The inanity of this friend business is only apparent if you really think about it, and even then it will fly clear over the heads of most people. Use that to your advantage. Become "friends" with everyone you meet and you will never have to date them.

Rule #6
Wait for sparks

Most of what we know about dating and relationships comes from the entertainment industry. This is not surprising, because we find dating and relationships, and portrayals thereof, extremely entertaining. It's a perfect match.

Sadly, those entertaining and educating us on these matters tend to fail spectacularly in their own relationships. It's ironic that these master teachers have such difficulty implementing their own great knowledge, but at least their personal failures provide additional entertainment. Serves 'em right anyway for being rich and beautiful.

Perhaps the most important lesson these sages teach us is that we are supposed to feel butterflies, sparks, chemistry, a veritable inferno of blazing butterflies when we meet The One. Under normal circumstances these sparks, etc. will be felt immediately upon first encountering The One. No words need even be exchanged; a mere glance across the room, perhaps a flirtatious smile as well, is enough to ignite the sparks.

Being rational people, we recognize that sometimes it will take a bit longer for sparks to fly. A clever opening line or a joke that induces laughter may be required, perhaps even a few minutes of witty banter. After all, relationships take time to develop.

If, however, you do not feel butterflies, sparks, or chemistry after an entire date, there is great cause for concern. If the person seems to be a great companion otherwise, you might want to give it another date or two, but after that you are simply stringing each other along.

Many happily married people will relate that they knew immediately upon meeting their beloved that this was The One. Everyone loves these stories. You deserve to have such a story as well.

In addition, once the sparks start flying, they have to keep flying. The entertainment industry never portrays a mundane aspect to relationships. A single awkward silence spells doom. An occasional fight is okay, since fights are also filled with passion, but there will never be a dull moment. So if your relationship is not filled with constant excitement, if it does not resemble the arc of a 90-minute love story on screen, then clearly you need to move on.

Don't bother getting to know someone gradually, working on a relationship, and showing affection in ways that don't ignite sparks. You're looking for an inferno, not a pilot light. And if it takes many years until you feel sparks – even if it takes forever – just keep on waiting. You deserve to meet The One who does it for you. When you meet him, you will know it. You just will.

Rule #7
Jockey for leverage

Every relationship is a power struggle, from the very beginning until the divorce settlement. To avoid being on the wrong end of the latter, make sure to be in control from the outset. Once you give up leverage in a relationship it's very hard to get it back.

Ladies: if a guy leaves you a message, don't call him back right away. You might even want to let him sit and squirm for two or three days before you get around to returning his call. This lets him know that you are busy, that you aren't too eager to go out with him, that you have options, and that you definitely aren't desperate. This makes you appear more attractive and desirable (especially to yourself and your single friends). Make him work. You're worth working for, aren't you? So make him work!

If he doesn't call you back, he clearly isn't worth your time. Obviously he doesn't realize that women have equal rights now, which means men should call them multiple times before women call them back.

If he does call you back a second time, then you have made him pursue you, and you now have the leverage. Congratulations!

If he calls you back more than a second time, then he is either a desperate loser or a stalker. Dump him.

Guys: don't call a girl too soon after a date to let her know you had a good time and ask her out again. That gives her all the leverage. Let her sit and squirm for a day or two, maybe even a week if you really like her. If she liked you too, she will start to worry that maybe you didn't really like her after all, she will become depressed, and when you finally call she will be surprised and delighted to hear from you. Bam! You seized the leverage.

Even if she didn't like you too much, you will become more attractive to her by treating her dismissively. She will start to wonder if she really is so beautiful and amazing that an ordinary guy like you isn't chasing her. She will start to think that you really have lots of options, and therefore maybe you aren't such an ordinary guy after all, and therefore maybe she shouldn't risk losing you so fast. She might even crack and contact you first, in which case she forfeited all her leverage. (Be careful, though. Women who forfeit too much leverage will overcompensate and try to seize it back quickly.)

Women would have you believe that they want a guy who courts them and calls them often. Nonsense. All this does is boost their ego, cheapen you in their eyes, and set you up to be controlled by them or dumped by them, whichever they fancy.

What most women really want is a jerk who intrigues them, a man who makes them work to gain his attention and affection. They want to think that if they work hard enough they can change you and make you want them. By working hard they are put in their place as women, which they secretly desire – they want a strong man. And by changing you they validate their true power as women. Why should a woman who supposedly can change any man settle for someone who isn't a jerk? Where is the glory in that?

Some might think that if men and women communicated with each other in a timely fashion as they do with people they care about this would facilitate an easier, more pleasant relationship. How stupid! Fall into those dreamy romantic notions and you're sure to get a rude awakening when you have no leverage at all. If all you end up with is a broken heart, consider yourself lucky.

It must also be noted that this principle applies to online dating just the same. If someone sends you a message, do NOT respond right away. This makes you appear like you are sitting around waiting for someone to contact you, and that you have nothing better to do but get back to them. Make it clear that if you respond to anyone, you are doing them a favor.

Finally, if someone ever proves themselves worthy of a date with you (or you decide to go out just to amuse yourself), don't compliment them or show significant interest. This too gives up your leverage.

The last minute of the date has more leverage up for grabs than the entire rest of the date put together. Make absolutely sure to give no indication that you enjoyed the other person's company. Don't even say that it was nice meeting them or thank them for treating you. Do you think being polite is going to help you win in a power struggle? It's just a sign of weakness.

Just part ways in a neutral, somewhat dismissive fashion that isn't completely rude. For example, just say "Goodbye". Saying "We'll be in touch" is acceptable if it's not too clear that you mean it. No matter how you orchestrate your awkward, unenthusiastic parting of the ways, just make sure that whenever you go out, you go out on top.

Rule #8

Hedge your bets

This one is for the ladies. The truth is that many of the coming rules will be primarily for the ladies. Some people will consider this sexist, but it is actually just the opposite. Isn't the ongoing liberation struggle all about women being treated fairly? Well, part of being treated fairly means being treated honestly, and that means some rules will be all about the women. Being treated honestly also means that we're not going to keep track of how many rules, and what percentage of each, apply to each gender just so we can pretend that everything balances perfectly. Why should it? Distorting the truth just to coddle the feelings of women would imply that they are hyper-sensitive, weak, and incapable of handling the truth. That is quite sexist and offensive!

Ladies, you need to hedge your bets. It's hard to meet a good man, let alone one who is good enough for you. Now, don't get discouraged; there are wealthy, successful hunks out there, and you should be able to reel one in at some point. At the same time, it can be difficult to stay optimistic after years of meeting losers with pedestrian jobs who try to win you over with character. So you need to be prudent and prepare for the long haul without the man of your dreams.

Nowadays you don't really need a man anyway. It can be convenient to have one, of course, but what does a man REALLY bring to your life that you can't get without one? Unless he's fabulously wealthy and promises a major upgrade to your lifestyle, the sacrifices you will have to make for him will far outweigh what you get in return. It's a bad deal, plain and simple. Even if you cash in with a divorce, it probably isn't worth the time and trouble. Hold out for a better opportunity.

These days, marrying an ordinary guy won't be worth it for you economically, his companionship will be more a bore and a responsibility than a benefit, and the only guarantee marriage will bring is that you have closed yourself off to a more lucrative investment opportunity. In the mean time, you are really missing very little while you wait.

Until very recently, the main impetus for women to stop holding out was their biological clock ticking away. Being that God is obviously female, it's still a bit puzzling why She unfairly pressured women in this way to settle for inferior men. Thankfully, technology has overcome this glitch in nature. Women now have a range of options for producing children without the shackles of matrimony or the presence of a man in their lives.

It is a good idea for women to start freezing eggs as early as possible. This will allow them to date with greater confidence and dump barely-adequate men without any nagging concerns of missing the boat. No longer do you need to go on dates hoping the man likes you and trying to please him – how servile! Now the onus is squarely on the man to impress you. Just the way it should be.

Some progressives might suggest single parenthood as the ideal option for today's liberated, powerful women, but it is understandable that some women might still harbor quaint notions about marriage and family. Don't feel guilty if marriage is still an ideal for you. Just raise your expectations really, really high, then raise them a little higher for good measure, and arm yourself with an alternative that is almost as attractive. Then you can date with power.

Indeed, the ultimate expression of womanly power is to bear a child without a father. No man can produce a child without a mother, and a single man would be hard-pressed even to adopt a child. So what better way to turn the tables on oppressive men than to produce children without them? What better gift to give a child than a childhood without a father?

All this said, it's best to produce no more than one child as a single mom. You only need one to prove the point, and after that the burdens of parenthood far outweigh the benefits. So definitely hedge your bets, but don't get carried away. Remember: at the end of the day, it's all about what's best for you.

Rule #9
Denigrate half the world's population

One of the best ways to stay single is to develop a negative attitude about the entire pool of people you might potentially marry. One might assume that such an all-encompassing negative generalization would be considered unacceptable, but, on the contrary, this shenanigan is generally met with warm laughter and commiseration. No doubt this is due at least in part to a "we are all in this together" mentality; if I am willing to accept your nonsensical notions about the opposite sex, you will accept mine, and we can help each other stay single. It's great when people band together to help each other like this!

It is far more socially acceptable for women to denigrate the entire male population than the reverse (presumably because it is natural for victims to loathe their oppressors). Once again the entertainment industry sets a fine example here, feeding us steady portrayals of men as arrogant, buffoonish, insensitive, unfaithful, and entirely superficial. If a man is portrayed as gallant and worthwhile, it is most likely a fantasy story about a world that does not exist.

The media also feeds us a daily roster of activism on behalf of women and achievements by women. Every time a woman accomplishes anything, anywhere, it is a newsworthy story that must be celebrated by all. This might resemble the way one would treat the accomplishments of a small child, but don't you dare think women are being grossly coddled. They are fighting for their rights, and each small accomplishment is a historic victory.

A woman who still respects men, let alone looks up to one in dating, chooses to be a slave, and deserves pity and scorn.

The sooner you can develop a negative attitude about men, while simultaneously defining your accomplishments in terms of a gender struggle, the better prepared you will be for dating and relationships. If you wait too long, you might be tricked by religion or your grandmother (who foolishly remained married to such an imperfect man her entire life) to not make such a big deal out of all this gender stuff, find a good man, and be his helpmate. Or you might meet a man you like who is not worthy of you and find yourself drawn into that outdated life as well, thereby robbing yourself of reaching your true potential.

This rule applies to men equally, though nowadays you have to be a little more subtle to avoid being branded a sexist. It is still fairly acceptable to complain that you can't meet a woman who is down-to-earth, not preoccupied with money and vanity. But since you and your kind have oppressed women for so long, it's best to keep these opinions to yourself and simply approach dating with a negative attitude about women. Assume they are just going to use you for a free dinner. If you approach a first date with this belief, you are far less likely to be used by the same woman for multiple free dinners before she dumps you, which she surely will anyway.

This rule is based on the principle of leverage that we discussed earlier, but it preempts the whole power struggle with a defensive fortress. Virtually the entire opposite gender is awful. The few good ones out there are already taken. When you meet someone new, assume they are not a good one who miraculously remained single until now. That way, you won't be fooled. And when they say something or do something that rankles you even slightly, you won't be disappointed. In fact, you'll be glad. You found out sooner rather than later that this person is awful just like all the other awful people of their gender, and you don't need to waste any more time with them.

Move it right along. There's nothing good to see here, anyway.

Rule #10
Go window shopping

Shopping can be an errand or a recreational activity, depending on your level of need. If you just got a hole in your last pair of socks, you go out immediately and buy some socks. You might not get the best price. You might not get the best socks. You're almost definitely not going to get the best deal on the best socks. But you're darn well going to get some socks. This shopping is an errand, and you need to make a purchase.

But many people like to browse around even if they have no particular need to purchase something, or if the need is eventual but far from urgent. Casual shopping is far more enjoyable. There is no pressure. You can shop around for the best price. You can compare similar items based on a host of minutiae. You can search as long as you want. You can wait for new and better models to come on the market. (You can even make a purchase, though that ends the game. Browsing after the purchase is far less enjoyable, and is more likely to cause buyer's remorse than validate your decision.)

It used to be that window shopping required leaving your home and gazing into actual windows. Technology has made it possible to window shop from home, or with your cell phone wherever you may be. You can scroll, click, and swipe, endlessly searching for something that catches your interest for a short period of time. What joy!

This same technology has also made it possible to go window shopping in your search for a spouse. Some dating web sites boast databases of hundreds of thousands of singles. Even with some rudimentary filtering, that is a lifetime of window shopping. An endless sea of faces awaits you, with banal tag lines beckoning your attention. With all these options before you, merely earning a click of your mouse to take a momentary closer look is an achievement. It is definitely a buyer's market.

Oh, that endless sea of faces! Those desperate calls for attention! I am beautiful. I am fun. I am cool. I am clever. I am mysterious. I am different…so very different than the endless thousands of other people all trying to be different, yet not so different that they come across as weird. All trying to stand out and fit in at the same time. All seeking the perfect pose, angle, lighting, and facial expression while appearing not to try too hard – to look their very best while appearing entirely natural. All trying to demonstrate that they are the perfect blend of serious and fun, or perhaps the perfect blend of fun and serious.

You get to place these faces in your little shopping cart, or save them for later, or reject them with disdain. You get to rate them and rank them, like them or tank them, block them or save them. Whatever you do, you will never make a mistake. The customer is always right.

Besides, whatever you might have rejected is easily replaced. These are not real human beings with souls, minds, feelings, and unique combinations of attributes, shortcomings, and quirks. These are just faces, poses, and tag lines, like tiny commercial advertisements for products you don't really want or need. These are little diversions to entertain you during a boring staff meeting, a bus ride, or at the end of the day when you feel like a little window shopping for something you will need eventually, maybe.

A shopper who decides he needs to make a purchase will not have the pleasure of categorizing and filtering products like a little Greek god toying with his minions. He will not have the luxury of endless scrolling and browsing, or waiting to see who might sign up next.

He will find a few people who seem good enough, compare based on essential criteria, and make a purchase.

Later he will be sure to have buyer's remorse.

Don't let that be you. Be a casual window shopper.

Rule #11

Get headaches

Inexperienced daters tend to agonize a lot more about the people they meet. In so doing, they waste a great deal of time and emotional energy before coming to the inevitable conclusion that they would rather remain single than commit to this person. One of the many benefits of experience is that you learn to reject people much more readily, without first tricking yourself that this might be The One.

Experienced daters also learn to gracefully excuse themselves from dates midway through a cup of coffee. While your partner may still be earnestly trying to get to know you and keep the conversation flowing, it is clear to you that this is not The One. There is no reason to continue this charade. Simply interject that you have a headache and you will be free to go.

Your date will never suspect that this is a fib and that he is the headache in the scenario. His feelings will not be hurt by your early exit, and you will not need to continue feigning even mild interest in his intolerable company. Everybody benefits. In fact, this maneuver is actually quite sensitive for the other person; if you let the date run its course you would only increase the likelihood of him falling in love with you and being heartbroken when he learns that his feelings are not reciprocated. Your sudden development of a headache and quick departure is an act of great thoughtfulness. It's a shame he will never know how deeply concerned you were for his feelings so that your kindness could be properly recognized, but that is part of the sacrifice a selfless person is prepared to make.

Alternatives for the headache include neck pain, nausea, drowsiness, or fatigue. Your typical pharmaceutical advertisement can provide additional ideas, but we recommend keeping it simple. It is much easier to feign a headache than sudden blindness, for example. One can also suddenly remember that he has to be somewhere else, or even arrange a fabricated emergency in conjunction with friends.

There is a small possibility that your date will be oblivious to your cue and attempt to steamroll ahead with the date. In that case it is acceptable to emphasize that your headache is quite bad and you really need to go.

If your date expresses too much genuine concern and produces high-dosage aspirin, then insists that you take it in his presence, chances are he is calling your bluff. That is extremely rude, especially considering how considerate you were of his feelings, and you can feel free to just walk out on him. Even on the small chance that he saw through your lie, he should have the good sense and social graces to play along. It's bad enough that he made you bored and uncomfortable enough to feign a headache; does he have to make you feel guilty about that too? Does he honestly think that it's more polite to carry the conversation along and be affable when he is clearly not The One?

But don't worry, the headache or sudden need to leave will work like a charm most of the time. You might feel some stress the first few times you do this, but that, like the headache, will dissipate seconds after you are released from the date. You'll feel marvelous.

Rule #12

Induce a breakup

After a few years' grace period, the prevailing assumption is that if you are still single, most likely there is something wrong with you or your methods. This will begin with "friendly suggestions" from people who say they care about you, but before you know it you will be subject to an avalanche of criticism from all directions.

This is unavoidable. You need to understand this and learn to cope with it. Otherwise the people around you will drive you crazy and then they will blame you for being crazy. That's a raw deal if ever there was one.

It is vital to learn how to keep the critics off balance without giving in to their relentless pressure to change this or that about yourself. You have to arm yourself with evidence that you are serious about getting married, that you are putting in an impressive effort, and that you are doing nothing obviously wrong to turn away eligible suitors. Mind you, even if you do this to perfection it will not stop people from scrutinizing you and looking for a flaw to pounce on. (You're not the only one who knows how to do that, after all.) But you will manage to stymie a great deal of criticism, and even get sincere sympathy.

Here is the number one tip to do this.

Even if it's true that just about everyone you date is way, way off, you can't always be the one to call it quits. No matter how much the evidence is in your favor, eventually people will start to question your role in all this failure. Even people who tell you that you are the greatest, and that anyone would be lucky to be with you, will not accept you turning everyone down. It's not rational, but it's a fact.

At the same time, you still have to show your glorious side on dates so that people will want you and you will have the leverage. Occasionally you can get away with shutting down on dates, or getting a headache, but most of the time you have to roll with it.

This is a very tricky balance. If you are too fun to be with, the other person will like you and will probably not want to end it. That makes you the bad guy. You will have to come up with a reason, and you will have a hard time fighting the inevitable charge of being "too picky". On the other hand, if you develop a habit of shutting down on dates, you will be accused of not giving people enough of a chance.

The key is to be subtle. Gradually suck the energy out of dates in ways that only an extremely perceptible person will ever notice. (You will not date enough of these people to harm your reputation.) Learn how to lead conversations into dead ends that aren't sudden. If your partner demonstrates a great deal of enthusiasm for something, always respond with significantly less enthusiasm, while still appearing positive and supportive. When he shares something interesting about himself, be polite, but don't make a big deal out of it. Keep your body language closed and distant. Master the art of being somewhat aloof in indescribable ways.

At some point your date will simply be unable to maintain a high level of energy, and you will be able to mutually agree that it was nice, but there was no chemistry. Every date that ends like this is an airtight piece of evidence that you are trying, there is nothing obviously wrong with you, and it is unfair to criticize you.

Another bulletproof strategy is to find something to be "concerned" about. Maybe he doesn't have quite as many friends as you do. Maybe you work a nine to five job, and he has flexible hours. You're concerned about how that could work out. Maybe you like to celebrate Independence Day in a big way, and he is more subdued about it. You get the idea.

You then share this concern in a way that suggests you really want to work through it, but you are not sure it is possible. This backs your partner into a corner. After all, you have a legitimate concern and you were open with him about it. You didn't break up with him over it. You've done exactly what you're supposed to do in this situation.

Now the onus is on him to demonstrate in a completely respectful manner that your concern is really not a big problem. Enjoy that little high-wire act, cowboy! If he really likes you, he may suggest that the two of you try to work through it, or keep trying in spite of the issue. That's noble, but if you keep expressing concern (while gushing appreciation) he will give that up quickly enough. At some point the mere fact that you are concerned will force him to become concerned as well, and then you're pretty much home free. Either you will mutually agree that you gave it a good try but it wasn't meant to be, or he will outright break up with you, which makes him the jerk who didn't want to try hard enough for a relationship.

Either way, you come out smelling like roses. You tried, you put your best foot forward, there was nothing about you that he didn't like, and yet he was the one who decided to end it. What a relief!

There are few things in dating that feel quite so good as successfully inducing someone to break up with you. The rewards will last a lifetime.

Rule #13
Be fashionably late

This one is pretty simple. If you show up on time for dates, it demonstrates that you are spending way too much time thinking about the date and preparing for it to be able to time it so well. This smacks of intensity and desperation. Very unattractive. You're also giving up some leverage right off the bat.

If you show up a few minutes late, you avoid all this, and also increase the likelihood of making the other person wait and fret a bit before meeting you. The waitee always has control over the waiter.

Some people like to call or text that they are running late

to show that they value the other person's time. Don't do this. And when do you finally breeze in, don't acknowledge your lateness, and under no circumstances should you apologize for it. You're busy, you're wonderful, it's a privilege to meet you, and you're worth waiting for.

Anyone who doesn't like it can catch the next train out of there. You can be sure he'll wait for the train. You deserve nothing less.

Have a negative dating profile

Dating in general is a big pain, and online dating adds new dimensions to this pain. Earlier we discussed the convenience and enjoyment of going window shopping online. Well, there's a flip-side to that. All the losers, jerks, and crazy people are shopping too.

Unfortunately there is little you can do to prevent these undesirables from browsing your profile and sending you a message. If you are female, chances are you will be bombarded with attention, most of it from unsavory sorts with ignoble intentions. You have my sincere sympathies. No one should have to deal with creeps, and it's frightening how many creeps there are out there.

The best you can do is try to deter the few such people who actually bother to look at your profile before copying and pasting their pathetic attempt at a greeting. Write something like "No creeps please!", or "If you are a pervert, please save my time and yours and don't contact me." Considering how effective this tactic surely is, it's a wonder it has not spread more widely. For example, banks could post signs stating "No robbers!" to let robbers know in advance that their patronage is most unwelcome. If it works even one time, it's all worth it.

But don't stop there. After making it clear that you are not interested in hearing from creeps and perverts, provide an exhaustive list of all the other people who should refrain from contacting you. This may include: married people, people who are not serious about a relationship, people who were previously married, people who were not previously married, smokers, drug users, short people, people who still live with their parents, people without a steady job, people who can't write a complete sentence, bald people, fat people, people with certain political views, vegetarians, non-vegetarians, people who don't know the answer to certain trivia questions, people who don't have a clever opening line, people who want to correspond for a while before meeting, and people who want to meet without corresponding for a while.

Again, these are just examples. Your "Do not enter" list should be as exhaustive as possible to save everyone time and aggravation.

After this you may want to include a similarly detailed list of prerequisites for contacting you. Make it clear that these are indeed requirements or at least very strong preferences. The more requirements you can "get out of the way" before exchanging a greeting, the less likely you will need to have an unpleasant break-up after exchanging two or three messages.

Your profile should also include a list of all the things you don't like about people, the world, the web site you are using, your profile, other people's profiles, and whatever else may strike your ire. People who dislike the same things you dislike will find this very attractive. What better way for people to bond than through hatred of people and things?

Don't worry that surrounding yourself with layers upon layers of barbed wire will create a negative aura about you that would deter someone worthwhile from contacting you as well. The right person will have no trouble seeing beyond the defense mechanisms and navigating through your minefield. Anyone who isn't eager to do that simply doesn't get you and is obviously not worth your time.

Rule #15

Have a boilerplate dating profile

It's fascinating that people readily share so much information about themselves on social media, yet when it comes to online dating they are suddenly so concerned about "privacy". People are such funny things.

There is a reason for this phenomenon, though most people never stopped long enough to think about it. If you stop to think about anything you might miss out on the latest updates and trends. Fortunately, I've done the thinking about it so you don't have to.

Social media offers virtual relationships, a platform where there is no need to meet a person for real, ever, to feel part of something. This vehicle is fueled by a mix of narcissism and voyeurism, a yearning to stand out, combined with a desperate need to fit in. On social media you can always look your best and sound your best, you can come and go as you please, and you can drift in and out of conversations and relationships with little accountability. You can feign interest and excitement in other people's lives with little effort, and receive the same token validation in return, all in your pajamas or your spare time.

In order to play this game, however, you do need to post content periodically just to stay on people's radar. The more content you post, the more active and interesting you seem, even if the content has little depth.

[In fact, superficial content is generally a much better idea. Depth by definition demands greater focus and thought, possibly even a change of behavior, and it is almost certain to be controversial. That is a cardinal sin on social media, where "offending" someone is the most serious crime one can commit that doesn't carry actual jail time (in some cases, jail time would be a less severe punishment than what the offender will suffer).

Perhaps the main reason why true depth and individuality of thought are so shunned on social media is because it threatens the very foundations on which this virtual universe is built – escaping the real world, real relationships, and one's true self. Many will vociferously argue that THEY have relationships of great depth on social media, and that the time they spend there greatly enriches their real lives. I posit that almost no one reaps great benefits from the virtual world without crossing into the territory of diminishing and negative returns, and the ongoing decline of real relationships in today's world supports my position.

For every rare individual who strikes it rich gambling at casinos there are countless others who lose on the bargain. Gambling one's time on social media is little different. There will be occasional small rewards, and a steady stream of intoxicating noise and entertainment that keeps one engaged, unable to disconnect even as his losses in real life mount.]

Suddenly our social media wizards are faced with filling out a profile for an online dating site. The purported goal of THIS medium is to discard it in favor of a real-life relationship infused with depth. That runs counter to so much of what the virtual universe is all about: escaping real-life relationships with all their warts and blemishes. Social media urges us to be "liked" by the masses, and that requires conforming. Dating web sites urge us to find one special someone from among the hordes, while simultaneously urging us to continue conforming to various categories, checklists, and algorithms that decide exactly who we are and what we need.

Somewhere along the way this stops being fun. Pretty soon, in fact.

The best way to navigate this challenge is to create a short, boilerplate profile that portrays you favorably without saying too much about you or distinguishing you from the masses. Play it safe! You can continue to feel that you fit in with everyone else who engages in this charade, and your dating profile will then become just another vehicle for the flighty, superficial banter that draws you to social media in the first place. You don't need to make yourself vulnerable, stand out, display any serious depth, or – God forbid – devote serious thought to who you really are as a person. Keep it simple and let the algorithm decide for you. If you don't like the results, just change your answers until you come out looking better.

There are numerous other benefits to this approach:

1) If you devote serious thought to creating a truly interesting and meaningful profile, you might discover that you are not really as interesting as social media would have you believe, and your life is not all that meaningful. Who wants to go down that road?

2) If you create a simple, boilerplate profile, you can get right to doing what really has you excited: checking out other people! Why look inward when you can look outward?

3) Most importantly, you get to convince yourself and others that you are doing what you can to get married. After all, only someone who really means business would do something as unpleasant as signing up for an online dating service. The very act reeks of failure and desperation. If you are willing to swallow your pride enough to do this, you have a powerful response to anyone who challenges your seriousness about getting married. They will not dare suggest that your boilerplate profile is a subconscious – let alone conscious – ploy to discourage people of depth from engaging you in a relationship filled with depth.

One final suggestion is to have no profile at all. Just post some airbrushed picture of yourself without any text. You still score points for signing up, but you invest no time or thought, share nothing personal about yourself, and keep all the dating leverage firmly on your side. You can contact those who strike your fancy, but you leave little opening for anyone to contact you. Anyone who tries is obviously a shallow person who only wants you for your good looks. What else could they possibly want you for, being that you offered nothing else? This doesn't make you shallow as well, of course, but it definitely proves that whoever contacted you is a creep.

At some point in your single career you will probably face insurmountable pressure to sign up for online dating. If you create a boilerplate profile you will minimize the discomfort and stay in control.

That's what most people are doing. Why be different?

Rule #16

Dwell on what could go wrong

The vast majority of attempts at a relationship don't work out. The more serious a relationship becomes before it blows up, the worse the fallout is likely to be. This alone is reason enough to be very, very leery of entering a serious relationship.

By avoiding a serious relationship you protect yourself from all of the following: a broken heart, guilt over breaking someone else's heart, a messy breakup, a messy divorce, alimony payments, abusive relationships, unplanned single parenthood, emotional baggage, and otherwise losing everything you invested in the relationship.

The risk you incur by avoiding a serious relationship is really quite minimal, since the odds of having a relationship worth the price of admission are stacked against you.

Clearly, serious relationships are a poor investment. The fact that most people continue to pursue them is testament to our deep natural need for them. Once again, nature gets in the way of what is best for us! Dwelling on what can go wrong with relationships, instead of being seduced by the wistful hope that it will go right, will help you overcome this.

Small-minded people will accuse you of having "cold feet" or "fear of commitment". This is offensive. These disparaging monikers refer to someone who is already in a serious relationship with the right person, but who runs away through misguided concerns. That's not you. If you were in a serious relationship with right person of course you would go for it! But you haven't met the right person, there is no serious relationship to commit to, and you are averting a serious relationship for entirely sensible reasons. Your prudence should be applauded.

Rule #17

Share worst date stories with the world

One of the greatest pleasures of dating is collecting horrible and bizarre experiences and sharing them with others. Learning to laugh at one's own misadventures is an important stage of emotional development. Few areas in life provide as much opportunity for this as dating.

When people first start dating they tend to take it much too seriously, which causes their initial frustrations to hurt much more than they should. (It takes time to grow layers of scar tissue, develop defense mechanisms, and close off your emotional openness in dating!) They will tend to share their bad experiences only with those closest to them.

What a mistake! The commiseration and support you receive from a few hand-picked confidantes is nothing compared to the laughter and approval you can receive by publicly sharing your worst dating experiences. Soon you will learn to look forward to bad dates rather than dread them. You will even begin to hope that boring dates turn bad so you will have more material. Bad is good!

Some singles blog about their bad dates, and the fortunate among them parlay their popularity into book deals. It almost makes you feel sorry for those who find the right one. If nothing else, finding the right one means you can only recycle old stories.

One of the best implementations of this rule is to share bad date stories at singles events. This has several benefits:

1) It's an excellent ice breaker.

2) It will show people how funny and interesting you are.

3) It sends a subtle message to all the losers in the room to avoid dating you, lest they become the foil for your next story or blog post.

Sharing your bad date stories publicly is entertaining and therapeutic. It will help you enjoy bad dates, while making you appear cool in social settings without making you approachable – a wonderful tool for singles to not get married.

Rule #18
Do lots of pre-date research

It is highly improbable that you will want any particular person you go out with. This might sound discouraging, but it's actually wonderful news. The less likely it is that you will want the next person you go out with, the better your chance of filtering that person out without having to meet him.

Dating is generally a thinly veiled interview process anyway. Interviews are not fun, and there is no need to subject yourself to one when you can filter out undesirable candidates preemptively. The more you research someone before going out, the better your chances of discovering why it won't work before having to discover this in person.

Some would recommend a careful balance of sensible filters with "taking a chance". Nonsense. This is one time you want to go to the absolute extreme. The last thing you want to do is waste time on a date with someone who isn't right for you. That could cost you an an hour or even a few hours of your life. If you spend a few days, or, preferably, a couple of weeks researching someone before agreeing to a date, you will save those precious hours.

To compound the savings, you can recycle the time you save into researching and rejecting other people without meeting them. If you continue to compound your savings over many years, without withdrawing too much for actual meetings, by the time you are fifty you will have enough time saved to retire as a happy single. The sooner you start saving, the better, but it is never too late to start.

Rule #19

Believe the hype

Children are typically raised in one of two ways. Doting parents will try to build the self-esteem of their children by frequently praising them and exaggerating their accomplishments. Less fortunate children will have parents who frequently belittle them or worse, failing to even acknowledge tremendous accomplishments, thereby destroying their self-esteem.

While the first approach is obviously more desirable and loving, it can also be harmful to the child. Parents who give their children an overdose of praise, while failing to deliver a deserved rebuke, are likely to handicap their child with an inflated ego. No one is born thinking he is better than every-one else. He has to be told that enough times to believe it.

By definition, the average person is average. The average person is more gifted than others in certain areas and below average in others, but the sum total of the average person is average. Society bombards us with messages that being average is a failure, that in fact being anything less than the very best is an embarrassment.

At the same time, incredibly, many parents and educators lavish praise on average or below average children simply to make them feel good, without regard for the long-term effects of accepting a mediocre effort. Rightfully concerned about damaging children's self-esteem, the pendulum has swung so far the other way that well-deserved criticism of young people has become taboo. (Oddly enough, the pendulum remains on the opposite extreme when it comes to adults, who are subject to merciless criticism for their failures, without concern for their feelings or the effectiveness of this approach.)

Feedback that is encouraging but also honest and to the point would help create people with a true sense of self and the motivation to be their personal best without getting carried away. This would only be good for the human race, but, being self-destructive as it is, most of the human race chooses dishon-esty, extremes, and conflicting messages in raising children.

There is one silver lining in all this: chances are you've had it drilled into your head from an early age that you are absolutely wonderful and that anyone would be lucky to marry you. No one has ever told you that you are ordinary and pedestrian, indistinguishable from your peers in most ways, and that in the vast sea of singles you're really just another fish. Better than average in some ways, worse than average in others, and overall…you're just plain average.

Of course not. You're a catch! Quite a catch! Catchier than all the other great catches out there!

Part of the responsibility of being so much better than average is to look down on most people. Average people with an inflated ego are adept at overestimating their own standing while selling others short. Of course, most people will be giving you the same treatment. The only difference is that YOU are right. You're terrific. They are nothing special.

Believing the hype about yourself will make it extremely easy and justifiable to say no, which, of course, is one of the cardinal rules for staying single.

Rule #20

Develop sharp radar

People tend to be on their best behavior in dating. Considering how poorly many people perform on dates, it's frightening to think that this is their best. But even people who bring little to the table can learn to fake it for a while.

It's important to keep in mind that the person you are dating is probably a loser or a creep in disguise, even if they seem pretty cool when you first meet. The sooner you can unmask the real them, the better off you will be. Like a nation defending itself from a stealth attack, you need to develop top-notch radar to detect threatening and unusual objects.

Some people approach meeting a new person with a positive attitude, driven by such quaint notions as "most people are good", "give people the benefit of the doubt", "judge others as you want to be judged", "and innocent until proven guilty". That is all well and good for the chapel and the legal system, but this is your future at stake.

These sunny sorts look for things they like about the other person and have in common with him. This forms the foundation of their relationship, providing incentive to work around the differences and dislikes that will inevitably arise. Sounds lovely and romantic until those differences and dislikes turn your life into a nightmare, and you wonder how you missed all the warning signs.

Most people are level-headed enough to spot obviously abusive or deranged behavior and terminate a relationship. But that is not enough. You need to learn to detect the subtlest of signs that there may be a problem lurking beneath the surface. You need to micro-analyze and psychoanalyze every little thing the person says and does to try to uncover the defects he is surely hiding from you. If something can be interpreted in a way that reflects negatively on his character or personality, you need to interpret it that way. It's your choice whether or not to give him a chance to explain himself, but do you really want to be with someone who does things that can be interpreted negatively and then has to explain himself? Whatever you decide, don't just let these things go.

The radar defense should be fully operational on the first date; the mere fact that someone passed the pre-date screening process does not entitle him to a breather. If you wait until later to start looking for what is wrong with him, you are sure to waste your time, and also run the risk of developing feelings for the person that will cloud your judgment. You might even decide to marry the person and even – God save us – stay with that person, faults and all!

Every time you overlook or dismiss something you don't like about the other person, you are just giving yourself one more reason to kick yourself down the road. The odds of that happening are infinitely greater than the odds of you thanking yourself for giving the person a pass.

Rule #21

Hold out for someone better

With all the talk about losers and creeps, it's important to remind yourself every now and then that there are quality people out there too. It's important to acknowledge this in dating as well; if you have nothing but scorn for everyone you've ever dated, it will reflect poorly on you.

We've already discussed various methods for wiggling out of relationships. These will only help if you have the proper attitude. Just because someone has good character, treats you well, shares your main values, is fun to be with, and is reasonably good looking doesn't mean you should stop the merry-go-round and marry the person. Many young singles make this mistake, and forfeit a lifetime of possibilities.

If they stopped to think they would realize that if they keep looking, they will eventually meet someone better. The odds of this person being the best possible match they will ever meet are extremely low. Sure, they can marry him and be reasonably happy, but isn't it worth it to wait and then be even more happy? Doesn't it pay to remain single a few more years so all the married years that follow can be even better?

Each time you meet someone who is better than the previous best, you should continue to raise your standards even higher. You've learned that your value is higher than you previously might have realized; you can probably do even better!

Inevitably you will go through stretches when you only meet people vastly inferior to your previous best option. This might cause you to get anxious and consider settling the next time you meet someone who is pretty good but still inferior to your previous best. This is one of the worst decisions you could ever make. If you settle now you will be acknowledging that you made a mistake by passing up someone better long ago, and you will have to live the rest of your life knowing that you wasted all that time AND wound up with a worse deal. Do you really want to live with that?

If you marry someone too soon you run the risk of missing out on someone better. If you marry someone decent too late, you will feel like a fool forever. Both outcomes are bitter pills to swallow. The only way to avoid them is to continue to hold out for someone better.

How will you know you met the best possible person and it's finally time to stop the search? Don't worry. You just will.

Rule #22
Have your priorities in order

Getting married means having a lot of responsibilities – to other people. That means less time for accomplishing your goals in life. It is much easier to accomplish your goals without the burden of caring for a spouse – and, God forbid, children. You already have family and friends to devote yourself to. Why take on these additional responsibilities that will tie you down and rob you of the prime years of your life?

Before getting married you need to accomplish all of the following: complete your educational goals, achieve a high-powered career, become fully independent, rise to the top of your profession, and make enough money to live comfortably. If you get married before all this you are selling yourself short.

However, the above is simply the bare minimum. If you are an ambitious person then surely you have additional goals. Maybe you want to travel the world. Maybe you want to write a book. Maybe you want to design a new product or start a company. You get the idea. Whatever it is you want to do in life, make sure you do it before you get married.

Getting married can also be on your to-do list, of course. But if you devote yourself to marriage you will be unable to properly devote yourself to everything else. Why sacrifice your other goals for marriage when you can delay marriage and have it all?

You only get to be young once. Before you let some man or woman chain you down, enjoy the world of freedom and opportunity that awaits you. At some point it will be convenient to add marriage to your résumé, but it should be one of your latter goals. Getting married too young will stymie your development. It is like voluntarily entering a prison cell before preparing your needs for the period of incarceration.

Don't be misled by married people who credit the support and encouragement of their spouse for making it possible for them to achieve their goals. Generally speaking they are just playing nice. They achieved their goals in spite of the presence of a spouse, not because of it. If they remained single all that time they probably would have accomplished a lot more.

Get your priorities in order. Live life to the fullest, then, if it suits you, find someone to enjoy it with. Marriage can wait. Everything else can't.

Rule #23
Be a cold fish

Dating is an emotional roller coaster. Roller coasters, while thrilling, produce unpleasant physical sensations. Dating, while thrilling at times, produces unpleasant emotional sensations. There will be highs, but those highs inevitably come crashing down.

Young people are always looking to get high one way or another. Since whatever goes up must come down, they wind up vacillating between euphoria and depression – often in very short spans of time, triggered by the smallest of events. A child can laugh one moment, throw a tantrum the next moment, then revert back to joy in the blink of an eye. This sort of wild emotional swing only intensifies during the teenage years, and, thanks to the ever-lengthening adolescence of our time, can continue indefinitely. Staying cool and rolling with the punches has gone out of style. We have to react and over-react to everything.

When people start dating they bring this emotional immaturity into the process, seeking immediate highs and wallowing in the inevitable lows. Emotionally stable people develop the ability to be excited when things look promising and disappointed when they don't work out without their whole world being shaken.

This is a good first step, but even emotionally stable people tend to get hurt. When things look promising – or even before that point – these folks are likely to open up to the other person and make themselves vulnerable. They recognize that a relationship can only succeed if both parties trust each other enough to make themselves vulnerable to one another, and are willing to risk being hurt. The problem is that they do this *way* too soon.

Dating is like two enemy countries at a negotiating table, trying to achieve long-term peace. (The fact that these two people have never been at war is irrelevant; war is only one salvo away at any time.) This needs to be a gradual process. If one side lowers its defenses as a show of sincerity or trust, it is inviting the other side to obliterate it. Lowering your defenses is the last thing you should do, if ever at all.

Before you make yourself vulnerable to the other person, you need to start with a show of strength (leverage), and make the other person prove that they are worthy of even being at the negotiating table with you, let alone receiving positive gestures. In practical terms, this means keeping your poker face on for a good long while.

Don't share anything too personal about yourself. Don't show genuine emotion. Don't tell the other person you like him or enjoyed his company. Don't thank him for treating you to something (especially if you're a woman – you're entitled to a free ride anyway). Don't smile when you meet, and don't part affectionately at the end of a date. For that matter, don't show affection during the date, either. All that does is plant a big bulls-eye right over your racing heart.

Practice aloof politeness, and eventually you will master polite aloofness. This is an interview, an entry exam, a screening process. Your decisions should be guided by cold logic, not feelings and emotions. You can always let the emotions out of the bottle, but once they are out you can't stuff them back in. So don't make yourself vulnerable until you are absolutely sure the other person has earned it.

A warm fish gets eaten. An ice cold fish stays fresh forever.

Rule #24

Stay within your comfort zone

If you want to stay happily single, you need to avoid things that cause discomfort. This includes pretty much everything involved with dating and relationships. Since you have to play the game, you can't avoid dating altogether, but if you are "reasonable" about what makes you uncomfortable you can get away with a lot.

Experienced daters will come under enormous pressure to try foolish things. It won't be called that, of course. It will be called such things as "being more open-minded", "giving people a chance", "trying something different", "being flexible", and "compromising".

If someone tells you to do any of these things in dating, it probably isn't a very good idea. If their idea were something reasonable, they would not introduce it with the suggestion that you are closed and stubborn and need to open up. The fact that they are doing this indicates that their idea is really a mad science experiment with your personal life.

Yes, we all know stories of people who took a crazy chance for love and it all worked out. That's why these stories get told – they are so rare and fantastic. Some people win the lottery, too, and that also creates wonderful stories. But playing the lottery as a strategy for earning a living is a different thing altogether. Taking a wild chance should not be a strategy for dating. (Stubborn people will dismiss this solid reasoning and give you "tough love" about your sensible approach. Just throw them a bone once in a while by doing something slightly outside your comfort zone and making a big fuss about it.)

Even though travel and communication have advanced exponentially in recent times, society will still accept your refusal to consider people who are "geographically undesirable". If you have to travel more than an hour to meet someone, they are geographically undesirable. If you live in a large population center you can work with even more narrow geographic boundaries. God put billions and billions of people in this world, and enough of them are already within that radius. No need for inconvenience here.

If someone's work schedule is significantly different than yours, forget it. There should be no need for anyone to shuffle their schedule to make room for dating. If the other person can't fit smoothly into your day and week, by definition he does not fit.

If the height differential is even slightly uncomfortable, move on. Again, there are billions and billions of people in this world. You should not have to be uncomfortable with a height differential even an inch or two outside your comfort zone.

These are just a few of countless examples of how you can use discomfort to rationalize your rejection of people who would otherwise seem suitable. Society is so preoccupied with comfort and what makes us feel good that you can play this card frequently and creatively.

Besides, since marriage is all about upgrading your life and feeling good, if anything along the way makes you uncomfortable, you shouldn't proceed any further.

Rule #25
Don't cheat

The more time you can eliminate from your prime dating years, the easier it is to remain single. Previously we discussed the strategy of taking a break from dating to eliminate large chunks of time. That's a great tool, but it has its limitations. The following strategy is bulletproof.

The moment you so much as agree to explore the possibility of dating a particular person, you are officially "unavailable". If anyone approaches you offering an introduction, just tell them you are "busy" or "in the middle of something". If someone asks you out, politely explain that you are already "taken". If you have an online profile, dismiss everyone who contacts you and even freeze your account. Refrain from attending singles events as well. How could you? That would be cheating.

This might sound ludicrous to grandparents and young children. The former lived in unenlightened times, and the latter are not yet capable of convoluted thinking. They would suggest that merely considering a particular individual, or even meeting a few times, does not constitute a serious relationship. If you had the opportunity to meet someone fantastic, they would urge you not to pass it up just because you shared a cup of coffee with someone else. Grandma might even regale you with the story of how feisty old grandpa swept her away from the man she was dating.

Old people are so cute. But don't take advice from them. They're old.

If you establish communication with a member of the opposite sex for purposes of dating, you are spiritually linked

72

to this person, and you have a moral obligation to remain entirely faithful to him. If you go out with someone for a cup of coffee and then meet someone else for a cup of coffee, you might as well have an affair. The only difference is the existence of a marriage, and that is a mere technicality.

Of course you have no actual feelings for person number one, nor are you part of each other's lives in any meaningful way. So what? Society will laud you for your seriousness about the dating process and your sensitivity for people's feelings. At the same time, you remain free of any expectations to date anyone else for the duration of this pseudo-relationship. The longer you drag it along, the longer you are free.

Here's how you can stretch out every part of the process. From the time you first consider considering someone until you actually consider him can take a few days. Then you can spend as long as two weeks researching the person to decide if it even "makes sense". Then you can wait a few days to actually call, and you can play phone tag for a week or longer before you even speak. Add another week or so before you can actually schedule a date, then a few more days before following up, play more phone tag, then throw in a few more days for "thinking it over". By the time you finally break off the "relationship", you might have been "off the market" for two months! That is *incredible* value for a single cup of coffee.

Then you can even take a break to recover from your disappointment.

Feisty old grandpa will tell you stories about how he took out one girl in the afternoon and another the same evening until he eventually met your grandmother. What a lack of seriousness! People who are serious about getting married don't even look at anyone else! It's a wonder she stayed with him for fifty years!

Take yourself "off the market" at the slightest hint of a potential date and milk it for all its worth. It's one of the best ways to enhance your reputation as a serious person while keeping dating to an absolute minimum.

Rule #26

Find something to disagree about

People like to pretend that they are open-minded. With all this open-mindedness, intellectual honesty, and yearning for truth, combined with unprecedented access to information, we would expect more people to discover errors in their beliefs. Yet somehow it is exceedingly rare for anyone to change their mind about anything, ever. The best our generation of enlightened intellectuals can muster is "tolerance" for other points of view; insisting that nothing is black and white, everything is gray;

there is no right or wrong, only different "narratives". There are no facts, only opinions. That's not an opinion – it's a fact!

In other words, if enough people start believing that one plus one is three, or that plant life should be protected as much as human life, we have no right to call them wrong. All religious beliefs must be considered equally correct (which really means that none of them are correct), all lifestyle choices are equally appropriate (who are we to judge?), and the only person on this earth who is evil and must be destroyed is one who believes there is such a thing as evil.

The murderer has a story to tell that is no less valid than that of his victim. He should be understood. Perhaps he is the real victim. Since something pushed him to commit the act, he probably is a victim too. Since most people don't like murderers, he is also a minority that should be protected. If he and his victim are both injured, the murderer shares an equal right to medical attention. One who disagrees should be condemned more harshly than the murderer himself, for he has no narrative. It's critical to have a narrative.

If someone expresses a point of view that, from a purely logical standpoint, might be completely absurd, we are not allowed to say that. Who are we to decide what is logical or absurd? The appropriate response is to "agree to disagree". Disagreeing is uncomfortable, but agreeing is enjoyable, and the wonderfulness of agreeing overcomes the awfulness of disagreeing, even if the only thing we agree about is that we don't agree. Agreeing to disagree is wonderful; disagreeing to agree does not exist.

The concept of agreeing to disagree really means shelving all further debate and search for truth, forever closing off the possibility of someone changing his mind. People only change their minds if they are wrong, and since there is no such thing as being really wrong, there is no need to con-sider it. Open-mindedness nowadays really means listening to another point of view, nodding your head respectfully, then continuing to believe whatever you always believed. Closed-mindedness means believing that anyone can be wrong and – more importantly – that those who are wrong should change. How offensive!

Since disagreement is such an unpleasant thing that reeks of a desire for people to change, one of the best escape routes in dating is to find something you disagree about. It is unreasonable to spend life with someone who does not validate you. If they disagree with you about anything, they are not validating you, and you should go cold on them immediately.

Those pesky grandparents would scoff at this notion, claiming that back in the day people got married even if they disagreed about very important things. The main thing, they say, is that they loved each other, were committed to each other, and wanted to make it work.

Best to nod your head respectfully and just feel sorry for the old codgers. It's not their fault the concept of agreeing to disagree was not invented in their time, just like so many other technological and societal marvels. One can only wonder how they made it in a world lacking tolerance, understanding, gray areas, and enlightenment like we have today. It's a shame they didn't get to enjoy the world of peace and brotherhood that we have today thanks to these intellectual achievements.

When you discover that the person you are dating disagrees with you about something, don't even try to work it out. If he changes his mind, he is a flim-flammer; if he sticks to his guns, he is stubborn and closed-minded. You don't want either such person in your life. If he agrees to disagree, that is best, and you can both agree to part ways amicably. You don't need to spend your life agreeing to disagree with someone, either. It becomes tiresome after a while.

You might as well start over with someone else, who will hopefully validate you all the time. Even though there is no such thing as right or wrong, you deserve for your narrative to be validated. This is one thing about which we can all agree.

Rule #27

See what happens

On rare occasions you will meet someone you actually like and who makes it through your initial defenses. Don't get carried away. Just because neither you nor the other person decide to break it off doesn't mean you should make romantic gestures to one another. You can always do that later, but once you start there's no going back.

The best mindset to have in situations like this is to keep going out just to see what happens. This means that you treat the other person politely and even show some interest in his life, but you don't cross the line to actually showing affection and becoming a meaningful part of his life. That's serious stuff, and it carries with it a serious risk of leading to marriage.

If it's meant to be, it will just happen. The romance will blossom all on its own. You will feel those sparks, as we discussed earlier. Intentionally trying to deepen a relationship is artificial and forced, and does not qualify as the true love you are looking for. True love is spontaneous combustion, not pouring lighter fluid everywhere and striking a match.

Generally speaking, it's best to break it off quickly if you don't feel it, but sometimes, for whatever reason, you might be willing to continue seeing the person for some time. Don't feel guilty about it. But don't invest too much of yourself into it, either. Think of the dates as something of a curiosity, a diversion from an otherwise banal existence. Don't try to make something happen. Wait for it to happen.

Chances are one of you will get tired of waiting before too long. That's fine.

At least you tried.

Rule #28
Panic

It's bound to happen; you're attractive, and smart, and fun to be with, and just so wonderful. You're going to go out with someone and he's going to like you. A lot. And he's going to let you know it.

This is one of the worst things that can happen in dating. After all, you haven't decided yet that you want him to like you. You hardly even know him! He hasn't passed all your tests! You don't have feelings for him! You're not sure that you want to wake up next to him, and raise children with him, and spend the rest of your life with him! And he likes you! A lot! This is way too much, way too fast!

There is only one thing you can do in this situation, and that is slam on the brakes, hard. You need room to breathe, space to think, and time to sort it all out. If he likes you too much more than you like him, you need to take the wind out of his sails. If he is feeling sparks, and you are not, you need to douse that little flame with a monsoon of cold water. Don't try to catch up and like him more. He needs to step back and like you less, until you are ready to let him like you more.

One solution is to take a break from seeing one another, so the unwanted romance will die a natural death. A candle that goes out is harder to light. However, this is a slow death, and it will drain your emotional energy. The best course of action is simply to prepare a speech about how your feelings are not on the same page, or something like that, and make a clean break. The only thing worse than dating someone who doesn't like you enough is dating someone who likes you too much.

Women will encounter this unpleasant situation far more often than men. Men tend to be more direct if they like someone, which sparks panic more than the subtle signals women are more likely to send. Women have also learned to stymie their romantic instincts and take longer to decide that they like someone, whereas men swing for the fences if someone catches their interest. But these are generalizations; attractive men will encounter their share of women who fawn over them, laugh way too much at their stupid jokes, and come on way too strong.

If you don't like the person at all, chilling the temperature is fairly easy, though still unpleasant. But if you do like the other person, only not quite as much, then it's time to panic. Otherwise you might decide to take a risk that could lead to a blossoming romance that you aren't ready for. Romance should only blossom when you are ready for it, the moment you give the word, not a moment sooner, and definitely not when someone else gives the word.

Guys, don't bring the girl flowers. Don't tell her you like her and enjoy her company. Don't ask her out at the end of the date. Don't give her direct compliments. You might think such gestures will demonstrate that you are serious and will open her heart to you. Wrong! It will have just the opposite effect. It will freak her out and turn her off. She's not ready for a relationship with you. Why should she be? You're just a guy. Remember that.

Ladies, don't feel bad. He'll get over it and find someone else to shower with affection. You need someone who gives you space, and plenty of it. If Casanova doesn't know that by now, it's a lesson he needs to learn.

Panicking is the most rational decision you can make.

Rule #29

Surround yourself with singles

A remarkable transformation tends to occur when people get married. After a very short time they forget everything about what it was like to be single, replace their single friends with married friends, and believe they figured out the secret to getting married just because they found someone to marry them. When a single friend shares the news that they are getting married, perhaps the appropriate response should not be "Congratulations" or "Mazal Tov", but "It was nice knowing you."

Psychologists should study why married people so often disassociate themselves from their single friends and begin to look down on those who "remain behind". Most likely the disassociation comes in part from the fact that people can naturally relate to those who share their current station in life. Since married life is different than single life in so many ways, it is natural for people to drift apart as their lifestyles become more divergent. It's unfortunate to lose a friend for this reason, but at least it is normal and understandable.

What is more difficult to understand is why married people develop a condescending attitude toward singles. Perhaps it is natural for people to want to believe that they are smarter and more deserving than those less fortunate, that they deserve all the credit for their own success. Suffice it to say that singles encounter a lot of condescension and unwelcome comments from married people who only think they know better.

There used to be little recourse for singles, but today they have formed "singles communities" to insulate themselves from the advice, criticism, and scorn that awaits them in traditional communities. Singles communities allow singles to avoid the discomfort of being unattached in a place meant for families. Why surround yourself with people who don't get it when you can surround yourself with people who do?

But that's not all. Single communities make it easy and fun to practice all the rules for not getting married in a safe, supportive environment! Whereas married people might call you on your shenanigans, there is an unspoken agreement among singles to support their own in remaining single. It's also common sense – their behavior is no more defensible than yours. Even the most hardened criminals have a code of honor. Singles play the game however they like and don't criticize one another directly.

The uninitiated might think that singles communities offer singles the best chance of getting married. After all, they offer the greatest concentration of singles and ample opportunities for them to meet one another. Some singles DO slip up and get married, it's true. But singles communities also offer singles the perfect environment for remaining single indefinitely. The vast majority of people you encounter socially will be single, and only a small percentage of them will be on a serious road to marriage. Those who do get married tend to disappear from the community shortly thereafter, and new singles who are in no rush to marry will constantly be joining to reinforce the ranks. The numbers will always be in your favor.

Another upside to living in a singles community is less frequent exposure to traditional family life, which might awaken a greater desire for such a lifestyle. That is not only painful, it can also reduce your fidelity to all the rules that will help you stay happily single. You might start to overlook obvious flaws in people you date and do more to achieve a relationship without delay. Obviously, this is a terrible mistake. Surrounding yourself with singles who are successfully remaining single will give you the support you need to do the same.

You will also be deluged with options, allowing you to look over the shoulder of the person you are with to see if there is a better option. Casual dating, where the idea of marriage is not even uttered until months or years go by, is the preferred norm. You will enjoy waiting for the next crop of singles to join the community every season so you can hunt for new blood. Traditional communities offer none of this.

Married people think they have it best and know best, and they will always be pushing you to enter their ranks. View them with suspicion at all times. Only your fellow singles will support your lifestyle and the decisions you make. Surrounding yourself with them will increase your chances of dating without the specter of marriage or avoiding it altogether.

What could be better than that?

Rule #30
Enjoy being single

There's a funny thing about pendulums, at least as they pertain to societal behavior. They tend to swing from one extreme to the other, spending very little time in the equilibrium position.

For the longest time singles were made to feel inadequate and unaccepted. When they fled to singles communities, they found support and validation among their own. There is safety in numbers, and it became safe for them to speak out against their place, or lack thereof, in traditional communities.

Some married people were receptive to the message – not

enough to reverse the evolution of singles communities and make them obsolete, but enough to bring the issue to light and lead to progress. Some traditional communities took steps to accommodate singles and be more sensitive to their plight, but these were baby steps. Perhaps it isn't really possible for them to fully integrate singles; some measure of displacement is inevitable for singles where couples and children are everywhere. At least some people got the message.

But the pendulum did not stop there. Once expressing alienation from traditional communities became accepted, it was only natural to challenge people's notions a little further. Why should singles ever have to feel inadequate? What is wrong with being single? The collective force of singles decided that all this talk about there being a "singles problem" was tantamount to declaring individual singles as problems that needed fixing.

How dare they! The singles collective rose up and declared that they would not be defined by their marital status. Singles did not have a void that could only be filled by another person. They were not incomplete, they were not missing anything. They were whole just as they were. They did not need a spouse to fully experience and enjoy life. Being single was not a problem or a tragedy, but a lifestyle choice, a perfectly legitimate option.

This push-back against not only married people but marriage in general made serious inroads. Singles became defiant at any suggestion that being single was less desirable than being married. Like so many other persecuted minorities, they demanded recognition and equality!

Since most married people spend more time complaining about their marriage than touting it, and are increasingly likely to eventually rejoin the population of singles, there was little for them to say. Only religious fundamentalists clung to their dogma that remaining single is a problem, and no one likes religious fundamentalists - not even other religious fundamentalists. Their voice was marginalized to the point where it is rarely heard and never seriously considered by more "progressive" people.

In addition, even supporters of marriage who counseled singles urged them to take advantage of their time as singles to do things that would be difficult or impossible after marriage: furthering their education, pursuing a new hobby, traveling the world. They told singles to enjoy being single. This was often said as consolation to despondent singles, but it made sense. Moping around didn't help one get married anyway, and being single DID provide certain opportunities, so why not take advantage of it? If one had no choice but to be single for a certain time, he might as well make the most of it.

This idea was a good thing. More of a good thing could only be a better thing! Singles took this entirely sensible idea of making the most of a less-than-ideal situation, and combined it with the new doctrine that being single was an entirely legitimate lifestyle choice. No longer would singles have to temper their enjoyment of bachelorhood with guilt and fear. No longer would singles have to worry about marriage robbing them of their freedom and opportunities. No longer would pressure to marry impinge on the pleasure of being single.

Thanks to this wonderful enlightenment, the playing field has been leveled. Marriage is far less desirable (unless one is homosexual, of course, or some other challenger of previously accepted norms), and single life is far more enticing and acceptable. For too long tradition prodded and pressured singles to marry, sucking all the joy out of single life. No more. Now traditionalists can get a taste of their own medicine and be a persecuted minority. The whole world is against them, and it's about time!

Listen carefully, singles. At certain moments when you fail to surround yourself with entertainment, distractions, and noise, you might feel a disruptive pang for a "life partner", a "soul mate", or some such anachronistic idea. This is a lie; there is no such thing. Marriage is nothing more than a lifestyle choice, one that is likely to fail and sure to present constant headaches. It may be convenient for a time, but it is an invest-ment that is dangerous and requires constant attention. Such investments are best made for the short-term only. Single life is a long-term strategy.

Remember: if you ever decide to get married, the party stops right then and there. No more late nights out with friends. No more planning a spontaneous vacation thousands of miles away. No more dumping partners on a whim or searching for new romantic intrigues. Now you have responsibilities. To someone else. Who is taking away your freedom and inde-pendence just by being there. Any fun you have now will be carefully measured and negotiated.

The more you enjoy being single, the easier it will be for you to adhere to the rules of this book. And the more you adhere to these rules, the greater your chances of remaining single, thereby prolonging your enjoyment.

Enjoy being single! It's not only an opportunity, it's a way of life.

SURVIVAL GUIDE FOR SINGLES

Introduction

Whether you decide to abide by the above rules or break them, you're sure to encounter difficult and awkward situations as a single. At times you might even entertain the notion of killing yourself or others. Do *not* do this. It is *wrong*, and it will only make things worse.

The only other option, unless you are extremely fortunate, is to learn how to live with pain, disappointment, frustration, heartbreak, anger, mistreatment, loneliness, isolation, disaffection, self-doubt, fear, guilt, confusion – and that's barring anything out of the ordinary. No matter how full your life is, no matter how much you enjoy yourself while being single, if you really, truly want to get married and it's not working out for you, it's going to hurt. A lot.

I don't have the magic answer for any specific person, and anyone who claims they do is a charlatan. The world is full of matchmakers, "coaches", therapists, counselors, religious figures, and armchair quarterbacks who are quick to take credit when their suggestions work out, but never take responsibility when they don't. Somehow they are always the reason why a struggling single had a breakthrough, but never part of the problem. That's not cool.

What I *can* offer is a survival guide for navigating the world of unwanted bachelorhood. The rules for how to not get married are a sharp critique of the shenanigans many singles engage in. Many singles unwittingly doom themselves and needlessly hurt others along the way, and they deserve to be called on this. At the same time, singles often live a lonely hell.

The survival guide is here to advocate for singles and help them survive this hell as long as they must remain in it.

Part of this is simply acknowledging and articulating the realities of being single. This alone will help in many ways. Young singles will learn to prepare themselves mentally and avoid self-defeating behaviors. Veterans of the dating world who are more unfortunate than self-defeating will receive the validation and support they deserve. Perhaps most importantly, this guide will give married people a better understanding of what singles go through. Because even though everyone who is married was once single, somehow they rarely seem to get it (more on that later).

Part of this is offering strategies and solutions for some of the issues facing singles, many of which receive little attention. Part of this is providing insight and perspective for approaching dating before one even begins to date.

And part of this is simply having a good laugh at the absurdity of it all. It's rough out there, and you're going to need a good dose of laughter now and then just to survive.

Chapter 1
Humble pie

I asserted at the outset that if you break the rules for not getting married, then you have a chance. That might not sound very confident. Indeed, a book called "How to have a chance to get married" is less marketable than one making a bombastic promise. I'd love to sell more books, but not if I have to lie to you. Anyone who claims they have the secret to getting married is doing just that.

We like to believe that if we work hard and do things the right way, we are guaranteed to be successful. This is understandable. It's much easier to be motivated when you are convinced that your goal is attainable, and it's discouraging to think that you might fall short no matter what you try. Very few people can put their heart and soul into something if they believe they only have a chance. But I'm here to tell you the truth. In the best-case scenario, that's all you have – a chance.

Let's consider a scenario that is less personally threatening. Most people want to get rich. Rich people write books and give seminars offering "proven" strategies for getting rich. Somehow, though, the only person who is guaranteed to get richer in this scenario is the person selling the tips. You can read all the books by millionaires and billionaires in the world, but how much do you think that will really increase your chances of becoming one of them? How much would you be willing to bet on that beyond the cost of the book?

One of the most common "tips" will be to save money (which is interesting, since extremely wealthy people are generally not known for their frugality and modest lifestyles).

Start by saving the cost of the books and seminars by these experts. Do a simple Internet search for "secrets" to getting rich, which costs nothing and will give you much of the same information. If you have an ounce of common sense, you will find it laughable.

One article by a financial planner advises people on how to get rich. His brainstorm? Earn more and spend less. Can't argue with that!

Secrets of the extremely wealthy include: working hard, not working too hard, listening to advice, following your heart, taking risks, treating people nicely, learning from your parents, doing what other successful people do, having a positive attitude, thinking differently than the masses, doing what you love, and looking to get good value for your money.

Taken in isolation, these suggestions can all sound sensible and convincing. That's because every good lie contains an element of truth. The truth is that, to a certain degree, all of these suggestions are good ideas. The lie is that they will make you rich.

Some of these suggestions directly contradict other suggestions. Obviously they cannot be a formula for becoming rich. Some of these suggestions are so obvious that one who promotes them should not call himself an expert or act as if he is revealing a secret. Others can lead to poverty just as easily as wealth.

Work hard: do you know anyone who works hard and isn't wealthy? Me too! Apparently hard work does not translate to wealth. A good work ethic is virtuous, and it often correlates to success, but that's all it does, and often it doesn't.

Don't work too hard: I'm all in favor of finding a healthy balance between work and other pursuits, but this is no secret to wealth, either.

Listen to advice: Did anyone ever give you bad advice?

Take risks: Risks, by definition, have a high likelihood of failure. Ask any gambler.

Treat people nicely: I heartily agree. But the saying doesn't go that jerks finish last. And nice guys don't necessarily get rich. Sometimes they get stabbed in the back.

Learn from your parents: Because they are extremely wealthy? And they are always right?

Do what other successful people do: Because if you duplicate what someone else does you are guaranteed the same results?

Have a positive attitude: Because thinking happy thoughts creates money?

Think differently than others: Because every different idea is a better idea?

Do what you love: Because every hobbyist makes millions off his hobby?

Get good value for your money: As opposed to getting ripped off? Gee, I never thought of that.

Again, all of these ideas have merit to a certain degree, in certain situations. Many of them can help a person become more happy, more wholesome, and achieve more, which in turn *might* lead to better financial results. But that's the point: these are not revelations, and they are definitely not secrets to becoming wealthy. The world is filled with people who work hard, work smart, treat people well, enjoy what they do, think for themselves, manage their money wisely…and struggle to get by.

The "secrets" these tycoons share would not sound impressive if they came from someone living paycheck to paycheck. But the possession of money affords one an air of sophistication and intelligence. If someone has money, people will listen to him. They will assume he did something special to become wealthy, he knows exactly what it is, and it can be easily duplicated by a different person in a different situation.

What complete and utter nonsense.

Every so often an extremely old person is interviewed and asked for the "secret" to their longevity. I'm waiting for one of them to be humble and reply that God gave them good genes and blessed them with a long life. Do they really believe that if they started life over they could expect to live to a hundred again? Does a billionaire really believe that if he started life over again with nothing he would become a billionaire again?

They do. They really do.

If someone argues that the rich person is an arrogant fool, that his "secret" for becoming wealthy is laughable, and that the average taxi driver understands the world better, he will be condemned for jealousy. The only people who can challenge successful people and get away with it are even more successful people. That is the way of the world.

It takes an extremely humble person to acknowledge that his success is more a blessing and a gift than his own creation. Such a person will acknowledge that things could easily have turned out very differently. He is not smarter and better than many other people who did things much the way he did and were less fortunate. Such an approach makes for a less interesting magazine interview, and will not translate to a bestselling book, but it is the real truth.

One should not have to be deeply religious to recognize that there is more to the mystery of why some people have a golden touch and others seem to have the deck stacked against them than can be explained by a how-to book. Many people believe that God has a rooting interest in sporting events, but can't accept the possibility that He manages the flow of wealth. Why the former is plausible and the latter unacceptable only highlights the extent of Man's ability to delude himself and ascribe powers to himself that he does not have. We don't control nearly as much as we like to believe.

The financial experts can offer excellent advice on managing money prudently, living within one's means, and creating a responsible plan. Many people can't figure this out on their own, and others need help staying disciplined and on the right track. How-to books and seminars on these topics will be helpful.

Similarly, a how-to book on increasing one's chances for a

long and healthy life will contain sound advice. Here too there will be few bombshells, but one can expect practical suggestions for improving one's lifestyle.

The bottom line is that no one has the secret to fabulous success in any area of life, because there is no such thing. No one can explain why some people who employ these secrets fail to succeed at all, or only succeed after a long series of failures, or unexpectedly tumble off their successful perch. Successful people are not necessarily smarter people or better people. We just want to believe that so we can make sense of a confusing world – and try to capture their elusive formula.

The same is true when it comes to getting married. There are certainly practical suggestions for putting one's best foot forward, how to treat others, and how to work on a relationship. But there is no secret whatsoever to finding the right person, or anything close, when one is ready to get married. If things turned out a little differently, many people who are married would still be single, and many people who are single would be married.

Married people have not figured out some elusive secret. Generally speaking, they met someone they liked, that person liked them as well, and they kept on liking each other long enough to make a commitment. They liked each other enough to work out whatever issues and differences complicated the relationship. The rest is just details.

Married people who find themselves single a second time cannot simply duplicate whatever they did the first time to marry again. If married people really figured out the secret, it should have the same results for them a second time. All too often it does not. Furthermore, no one can predict with any accuracy when things will work out for a single, regardless of what strategy he employs. There is always that "x factor" of things coming together that cannot be predicted or explained.

A book claiming to contain the secrets to getting married is less valuable than a book on how to fix a drainage pipe. Only the latter contains suggestions whose results are provable and assured.

The first step to truly surviving the madness of dating, and, really, the world at large, is to eat some humble pie. If you are blessed with talents and success, don't delude yourself into thinking that you are the source of the blessing. It's okay to take credit for effort and sincerity. But that's really about it. Even if you really are smarter than the next person, you didn't have to be born that way or given the opportunity to learn what you know.

If you meet someone special and forge a relationship with that person, never forget how fortunate you are. It didn't have to work out that way, especially not for a dumb schmuck like you.

If you stay humble, I can't guarantee your success will continue. But I definitely like your chances.

Chapter 2
True success

Success can often be traced to a key moment, a crossroad, a series of dominoes falling in just the right way. That "chance" meeting could easily not have happened. It could have turned out very differently, too. The most one can do is seize an opportunity, but the results are never in one's own control. You can nail the interview and still be turned down for the job. You can bring your best self to that date, but the other person might still reject you. Their reasons will have nothing to with your performance.

How many athletes languish on the bench, knowing they are better than those on the field, but for one reason or another never get an adequate chance to prove themselves? How many people toil away for a company, watching inferior colleagues get promoted while their own achievements are never properly rewarded? How many talented writers, artists, and actors never land their big break, while others are "discovered" by some unusual turn of events?

We like to believe that everyone receives just the right station in life according to their efforts and abilities. But life isn't really fair. The best people don't always rise to the top. If they did, the world would be a much better place for everyone.

This idea is uncomfortable (especially if you don't believe in God, Who has a master plan), but in a way it is also liberating. It allows us to focus on that which *is* in our control – the process – and not be shackled to results that require an "x factor".

If we determine success based on fame, fortune, and accolades, then success is more a product of luck, access, and the whims of others than one's own effort and personal qualities. We are declaring pompous fools to be successful just because they got the break or knew the right people, while those who labor at menial jobs without fanfare are losers. We are also consigning our own self-worth to "fate".

If, on the other hand, we define success based strictly on how well we do our jobs, and leave the results to God, we can have true inner peace even if we are unsatisfied with the external results. (A person of perfect faith will be completely unperturbed by external results, but few reach that level. The more faith we have, the less we will be perturbed by things we can't control.) When it comes to any goal a person has, he will consider himself successful if he did what was reasonably within his domain to achieve that goal.

This is no way contradicts hard work and pushing oneself beyond what he thought were his limits. It absolves him from taking desperate, self-destructive measures to try to achieve his goal, and frees him from the stigma of failure if things don't work out despite his best efforts. We cannot fault someone for trying his very best, reaching his limit, and being unable to achieve something that was impossible for him or otherwise denied him by forces beyond his control.

For example, we tend to praise people for "fighting" and "beating" serious illnesses. Many people succumb to serious illnesses despite doing all they can to survive. These people are not failures in any way. We are mortal, and we are limited. Similarly, one who works hard and works smart but does not achieve wealth is not a failure in any way, nor is a talented person who never was "discovered".

Some singles, for whatever reason, are unfortunate in their efforts to get married. Their prolonged single status is not evidence that their efforts or their person are seriously flawed. You can only marry someone you meet, and you cannot control how and when you will meet someone suitable. You also cannot control how the other person will react upon meeting you. Sometimes the other person will not bring their best selves to the meeting, or will not be open to a relationship at that time. You can do everything right, but if the other person is lethargic or disinterested, it probably won't work out.

Married sages like to warn singles about the possibility of meeting the right person and turning him down for a trivial reason, perhaps never to have such an opportunity again. But they fail to address the other side of this story. What if the person they are lecturing did not turn down his intended, but was on the receiving end of the rejection? What do we say to the victim? How do we console him? How can we really be sure that the single under scrutiny is not actually the victim of an overly picky soul mate instead of the other way around?

Again, I have no solution for a specific individual who has been dealt a difficult hand. As a religious person I can suggest soul-searching and prayer, but I cannot guarantee a change of fortune. What I can offer is an honest, fair definition of success and failure that focuses on the process, not the result.

Someone who goes on dates with the proper intentions, treats people well, tries to see the positives of those he meets, and tries to make it work is dating successfully. I hope such a person is fortunate enough to meet someone in his ballpark who approaches dating the same way, for they will make each other very happy and build a beautiful home together. If, for whatever reason, he is not so fortunate, he is still dating successfully. He can look himself in the mirror and be pleased with what he sees. He can feel inner peace with himself and his efforts. He can ignore unfair criticism and calls to change this or that about himself just because "his way isn't working".

Someone who engages in shenanigans might well get married sooner, and it's even possible the marriage won't go up in flames. Such a person achieved marriage despite his approach, not because of it. His success is a gift, not something he can personally take credit for (though surely he will). Singles should not emulate his approach, nor be swayed by his self-righteous lectures about what they are doing wrong. He doesn't really know better. He just got a break.

Redefining success is not a psychological ploy to help us cope with disappointment. It is a perspective on life. Give yourself credit for trying hard and overcoming your personal challenges. Take pride in what you do. But don't define success and failure on whether you achieve goals that require an "x factor". You might not get that break, that job, that opportunity, that recognition, or even that girl (or guy). At some point none of these things are really in your control.

All you can control is whether you show up where are supposed to be and give it your best shot. Even if the results you want are late in coming – even if, God forbid, you never see the full fruits of your labor – you will have inner peace. This won't eliminate pain and frustration. Those are part of life. But the more you internalize this perspective, the less you will be deterred by such things. You will be more focused, more confident, more resilient, and more satisfied with yourself. You will make changes only because they are warranted, not out of desperation or to please others.

You will be a success. As a fringe benefit, this will improve your chances for achieving all your goals.

Chapter 3
Becoming an "older" single

There is a certain point in the aging process of a single when the people he always trusted turn against him. If you have been married for some time now, and have already forgotten what it can be like for singles, you're probably feeling defensive about that statement and presuming there is something wrong with the person who wrote it. If, on the other hand, you're single and have been for longer than you ever hoped to be, you know exactly what I'm talking about.

This transition in the life of a single is fascinating. Many things change during this period, and singles react to these changes in different ways based on their social environment and their personalities. Many of these changes are subtle; both the single and his former supporters may be unaware of what has changed until well into this process. The single, who bears the brunt of these changes, will pick up on it subconsciously at first, and later will experience a great deal of inner turmoil when it really sets in.

His former supporters, on the other hand, may remain oblivious to these changes forever. To them, nothing has changed, everything makes perfect sense, and of course they never betrayed the single. How absurd! They continue to support him as much as ever. He just doesn't appreciate it. That's part of the problem.

Let's explore this transition, what results from it, and what it really signifies beneath the surface.

When singles first start dating there are certainly nerves and fears, but the prevailing feelings tend to be optimism and anticipation. The notion that a young single might turn into an old single is distant from anyone's mind – a subconscious concern at best that will be quickly dismissed if actually expressed. This comes despite the ever-increasing prevalence of struggling singles in our time. We all want to believe that it can't happen to us, it won't happen to us. Proceeding with anything less than absolute certainty that it will all work out, and soon, is even seen by many as a religious failing.

This optimism runs so high at first that young singles who think they found the right person very quickly are often *discouraged* from proceeding. They shouldn't be hasty…they shouldn't settle…they should explore their options. Mind you, that is all sound advice, but when this advice is automatic it is not really advice at all – just noise. Noise that can confuse a young single and possibly spoil a relationship that should proceed.

Compare this to what those same people would tell the same single ten or twenty years down the road if he is feeling optimistic about the person he is dating. Don't blow it! Be willing to settle! Don't waste any more time!

Once again, that is sound advice, but not if it is automatic. This sort of noise can push a sensible older single to proceed with a marriage that will turn out disastrous.

The only difference between these two scenarios is the age of the single and the perception people have of him because of it. If a young single turns someone down he will rarely be accused of being foolish, narcissistic, or overly picky. The people in his life will assume that there are many other quality opportunities right around the corner, there is no cause for concern, and there is nothing disturbing about his approach to dating.

If an older single turns someone down, the immediate assumption is that he has made a poor decision. Again, the only thing that has changed is the age of the defendant and the perception people have of him.

Support or criticism of the decisions of singles is often based not on the merits of the actual decision and the thought process behind it, but on the age and resulting perception of the single. Of course this is entirely corrupt. Young singles should not get a free pass for bad behavior and poor judgment, and older singles should not have such strong bias against them.

I experienced all this first hand, as have all the other singles out there who did not get married by the expiration date stamped on them by their family and society. Growing up I was never warned that if I didn't change this or that about myself, I would have trouble getting married. When I started dating, if a girl was not interested in me there was no inquisition into what I must have done wrong to turn her off, and if I was not interested in a girl my judgment wasn't impugned.

After a few years went by without success, some concerns started to be expressed, but they were mild. I was a late bloomer. I was still a baby, in fact! It was only a matter of time until I found the right one. Maybe my soul mate was still too young to get married and I had to wait for her to come of age.

As time went on those supporting me continued to dwindle. It became much more popular to try to fix me instead. And oh, was there suddenly so much that needed fixing! Everything from the way I dressed, to the the places I went on dates, to what I talked about on dates, to how I expressed myself, to what I shared about myself, and dozens more things great and small. You name it, it needed fixing.

Mind you, *none of this* needed fixing just a short time ago, but now that the hounds were out hunting for flaws to fix, there was nothing that wasn't broken. How did I go from someone who was simply waiting for his soul mate to come of age (an ever-decreasing possibility) to a personal wreck who needed coaching, psychotherapy, rabbinic guidance, cemetery prayers, proclamations from kabbalists, and good old-fashioned tough love? And why were there no warning signs when I was younger? If I had so many obvious flaws that were holding me back from getting married, why did they only become issues after a few years of unsuccessful dating?

A single who is trying to convince his former supporters that his approach to dating is fine might as well hire a battery of lawyers to defend him. As this transition develops, convincing those he used to trust that there is nothing seriously wrong with him will go from difficult to utterly impossible. Bottom line: he is single well past the age when he was expected to be. There must be something wrong with him or his approach. Case closed.

At first a single will be blindsided by the betrayal of those he used to trust. Many of them knew him his entire life and never expressed such sentiments to him before. How could they suddenly think so poorly of him? Why was he suddenly such a loser in their eyes? What happened??

He will be sure this is all a simple misunderstanding, and he will attempt to defend himself. He will explain why he made certain decisions, why certain situations didn't work out differently, and why his lack of success to this point is not proof that his entire methodology is wrong. He fully expects those who know him so well to understand him and resume supporting him.

How wrong he is.

His attempts to defend himself will only be used against him, taken as further proof that there is something deeply wrong with him. On top of all his previous faults, he is now declared stubborn, oblivious to faults that are apparent to everyone else, and unwilling to accept constructive criticism. Of course such a person cannot get married! Who would want to marry someone like that?

This is the moment when darkness descends on the single. He now realizes just how alone he is on this journey. As his former supporters will conspire behind his back to save him, the single will take stock of his family and friends to determine if there is anyone left he can still confide in without have the tables turned on him. Odds are high that the only such people will be fellow singles. And even there his support will be lukewarm; even singles are skeptical of one another, and it's always easier to criticize than to support. Who wants to climb aboard a sinking ship without a crew?

As this realization sets in the single reaches a critical crossroad. What will he do now? He has only the following few options, none of which are pleasant:

Option #1: Continue to defend himself against his detractors and stick to his guns with his approach to dating. This will seal his fate in the eyes of those who betrayed him, and will guarantee an unending stream of "constructive" criticism from them, with hopes of finally "getting through" to him. The accusations against him will only become more extreme as time goes on, his catalog of flaws and failings that impede him from getting married will continue to grow, and those who betrayed him will rarely if ever acknowledge anything positive about him in this aspect of his life. It doesn't matter what he does or doesn't do. Until he breaks and does whatever *they* tell him to do, he's wrong.

Relationships that used to be dear to the single will be strained and sometimes frayed beyond repair. He will experience emotional trauma during this process, and will at times question himself amid the storm of criticism from near and far. Can they really all be wrong? Should he really be so sure of himself? And even if he should, is it worth it?

In movies we all admire the lonely bearer of the truth who courageously journeys onward, refusing to surrender to the howling masses. In real life we scorn him. And we would certainly not want to *be* him. Therefore, very few people respond in this way, and those who do usually give it up before too long.

Option #2: Surrender. You can't fight the whole world, and few people want to marry someone who is valiantly engaged in such a hopeless battle. It's much easier to give in, fit in, play the game, and be part of the system. You don't have to like it. If you catch people in an honest moment, most of them will agree that they hate it all as much as you do. If you go along with it anyway, you can date and potentially marry other people who have surrendered. If you stick to your guns, the people who surrendered will be afraid to associate with you, even if they admire you.

So you can either be a hero who repels even those who share his feelings, or surrender, do what the gatekeepers tell you to do, and then be accepted. For most people this is a very easy choice. Almost everyone will choose to be a slave to a society they don't especially like rather than a pariah who insists on being true to himself. If that means changing to fit in, and continuing to change according to the whims of others, so be it. If that means eroding their true selves to maintain conformity, erode away.

Most people surrender to societal expectations shortly after birth, so they transition easily to this mindset when they begin dating. Those who try to be genuine and true to themselves will face a crushing response from peers and educational institutions. Usually this is enough to set them straight. If more help is needed, government intervention is available in most parts of the world.

Option #3: Rebel. Many singles are driven by the pressure and criticism to rebel against their society of origin. This may include downgrading or abandoning one's religious observance, becoming more promiscuous, and even discarding the idea of a traditional marriage in favor of an "alternative" lifestyle.

When one's community fails to support him – or rejects him altogether – he will naturally seek support elsewhere. Modern technology and communication have made it much more difficult for insular communities to keep people in the fold through fear alone. If they do not offer support and acceptance, only the most committed and successful members will stay. Communities that pressure singles to marry, and punish those who remain single with stigmatization and ostracism, will lose many of these singles to more welcoming communities. At some point almost everyone is bound to crack.

Many singles with a strict religious upbringing, after years of disappointment and disillusion, even feel compelled to marry out of their faith because it seems to be their only option. While I cannot condone this, I can certainly understand it. The first comment God makes about the human race is that "It is not good for Man to be alone." How awful it is for one to feel he must choose between being a religious disgrace and being alone.

Rebellion against one's society of upbringing is not a first choice, but a last resort. However much he failed his society, his society likely failed him as well.

Most singles vacillate between these three reactions to varying degrees. Those who surrender more in the beginning will become hardened and defiant as time goes on. Those who are naturally more stubborn or rebellious may become worn down and surrender.

Becoming an "older" single is painful enough without external pressure, criticism, and guilt from loved ones and one's society. If everyone involved will eat a little more humble pie… if they will redefine success to be loving toward well-meaning singles… and if they can welcome and support those who are struggling, a tremendous amount of needless suffering can be avoided.

I believe any reduction in the awful pain felt by older singles will help them get married; depression and disaffection are not attractive qualities. But even if improving the way we relate to older singles would not help even one person get married one day sooner, it is incumbent for its own merits alone. Singles should know that they can confide in those close to them, and receive acceptance, support, and love – even if their methods are less than perfect.

Betrayal is one of the worst things a person can experience. Singles experience this so often that they are compelled to choose between betraying themselves (changing to suit others) or betraying their community in return. At some point they become little different than victims of abuse, who find it difficult to trust anyone, ever. Is this something we want singles to bring with them into dating?

Singles who become "older" are forced to do a great deal of soul-searching. It's time their married friends and loved ones who betrayed them did the same.

Chapter 4
Mental health

One of the rites of passage in the aging of a single is the inevitable suggestion that he "talk to someone" to figure out why he's having such a hard time. Those less tactful will suggest he figure out what is "blocking" him from getting married. The unspoken assumption is that anyone who really wants to get married and has nothing seriously wrong with them can do so whenever they wish. Therefore, those who remain unmarried beyond the expectations of their society must be doing something wrong or have a psychological block that prevents them from getting married.

The possibility that the single is fine just the way he is and simply needs to meet the right person will expire around the time this suggestion is first made. The possibility that the society itself bears any responsibility for the difficulties facing the single will not be considered. After all, people will counter, many other singles from the same society are getting married. So if anyone is having a problem, it must be with them.

Also, it is much more convenient to suggest that individuals go for help than for an entire society to look itself in the mirror to determine why so many of its members need intervention.

Once again, it's interesting that no one makes this suggestion to young adults before they begin dating. If they really had such obvious psychological issues that would prevent them from getting married, one would have expected these issues to manifest themselves long before the single became "old". Why didn't anyone suggest an ounce of prevention to save years of frustration? Why can't all these armchair quarterbacks look at a high school class and predict who will remain single if they don't get help?

I'll tell you why. Because they don't have a clue what they're talking about.

Mind you, many people do have serious issues, and would benefit from some form of counseling. Even people without serious issues need guidance from time to time. There is also no shortage of married people with serious issues, which somehow didn't "block" them from getting married. Considering the great number of people with rocky and failed marriages, I don't think it's fair to assume someone needs help just because they are single. Another slice of humble pie, please!

Singles, like everyone else, should be honest and introspective enough to seek guidance for the challenges they face. But I would strongly recommend against bowing to pressure and going for therapy or coaching just because you're single longer than your society considers "normal". This is not evidence of a problem with you. It is not even reason to believe there might be a problem with you, and that an investigation is needed.

If there really is a problem with you, it should be apparent independent of your marital status.

If you are unsure whether or not the people suggesting you seek psychological help are blowing hot air, consider the following. If you announced, much to their surprise, that you have met the person of your dreams, would their reservations about you instantly disappear? If you really had a problem, this sudden good fortune should be irrelevant to the need to address it. If anything, it should only provide additional motivation to address the problem lest it interfere with this promising relationship!

Funny how the good fortune of meeting someone makes all those obvious psychological issues just disappear!

Furthermore, if those same critics who back off when you are in a promising relationship get right back on your case if it ends, they have lost any shred of credibility. They are simply jumping on and off the bandwagon, and should be ashamed of themselves for kicking you when you are down. Oftentimes the people who do this will be those closest to you, which makes the sting of their flippant advice and lack of reliable support all the more painful.

They really should talk to someone about that.

What of these dating coaches, anyway? This relatively new cottage industry of certified non-therapists makes a business out of helping singles figure out what is wrong with them. In the entire history of this non-profession, not once has a single ever gone for a consultation and been informed that he does not need the services of the coach, for he is doing everything fine and should just stay the course. (There are rumors about one such coach who told people that, but he quickly went out of business and could not be found for comment.)

There is a phenomenon unique to the human race that we must get our fingerprints on something in order to feel validated. If our livelihood depends on making this imprint, all the more so. Doctors are known to prescribe medication even when it is not needed; therapists rarely seem to "cure" someone and suggest he never return for more paid session; rare is the editor who takes a hands-off approach to even the best writing. When someone comes to us for advice, we feel better about ourselves offering advice, any advice, rather than saying that the person should stay the course.

Again, I say this as someone who believes that we can all benefit from advice and guidance. However smart we may be in one area we are clueless in another, and it is easy for us to delude ourselves. But those seeking advice should be careful, and those offering it should be even more careful.

The people around you will drive you crazy, then they will urge you to get help for being crazy. You're going to need a lot of fortitude to withstand this, and you will probably need to cut some people close to you out of your personal life. The coaches might call this setting boundaries; they like to give names to things.

Definitely set those boundaries, and don't be too quick to let armchair quarterbacks, paid or unpaid, inside them. You will need strong boundaries to survive as a single when the world starts turning against you.

Chapter 5
Everyone's a used car salesman

I have a great girl for you. She's pretty, smart, and fun. No, I didn't meet her, but she's my friend's sister-in-law's cousin, and she said she's really great. She told me about her and she sounds perfect for you. What else did she tell me? That's it, but you'll find out more when you meet her. Don't worry! She's fun, she loves to laugh. Oh, she also said she's nice. You want a nice girl, right? I told you, she sounds like a great idea.

You're going to hear variations of this sales pitch until you are jaded, cynical, and incapable of being excited to meet some-one new. Then you will be criticized for being jaded and cynical. But look on the bright side. The world is full of corruption, kangaroo courts, and despotic regimes. If things were a little different you might be flogged, incarcerated for many years, or even executed. Your unfair punishment – an intrusion of idiots into your personal life – is still unpleasant, but don't complain too much. These are benign idiots. It could be a lot worse.

When you first begin dating, even the most primitive sales pitch will be exciting. It won't occur to you that this might be false advertising, that the salesman might be clueless or have an agenda that doesn't prioritize your best interests. After a few disappointments, you will still maintain a measure of hope in humanity. You will decide that the first crop of salesmen meant well, but just didn't know you well enough or have the right information. You will start to ask more questions, but you will still trust the answers, and when you encounter resistance at your need for more information you will back off.

After you suffer more disappointments, including being flat-out lied to and otherwise mistreated, you will grow some layers of scar tissue. You will begin to receive sales pitches with suspicion. But you will still trust some people, either because you believe they know you well and care about you, or because they have a particularly polished sales pitch that addresses your immediate concerns. This will set you up for greater disappointments. These people will bore right through your scar tissue, rip your flesh wide open, wound you deeply, then leave you there to bleed. This is bad.

Fortunately, the scar tissue will grow back, stronger than ever. When the salesmen come calling again, bright and chipper as ever, you will smartly reply that you've heard their speeches before. You're a smart consumer now. You're going to challenge the sales pitch now. "What do you mean she's pretty, smart, and fun?" No one's ever offered to fix you up with someone ugly, stupid, and boring, yet somehow they've done just that.

You're not buying so fast anymore. You need substance, not platitudes.

You might choose to be polite. Maybe you believe in giving salesmen the benefit of the doubt no matter how many times you've been burned. Maybe you don't want to be perceived as difficult and confrontational. Maybe you believe this person deserves a parade in their honor simply for "thinking of you" and for "trying" – even if there is little evidence of any intelligent thought process or actual effort on their part. Maybe you simply haven't lost all your faith in humanity (what's it going to take?).

You will try to explain why you are skeptical when someone on the fringes of your life, or someone with a poor track record of fixing you up, claims to have a great idea. You will try to explain, in non-offensive terms, that their sales pitch really doesn't tell you anything meaningful about the person, that you don't think they have a good handle on who you are and what you are looking for, and that you need a reason to be confident that their suggestion makes any kind of sense.

You will expect the salesman to be understanding, sympathetic, and sensitive. You will be making a big mistake. Few salesmen will even pretend to be these things for more than a few exchanges in the conversation. They don't like smart consumers and they don't want to be your friend. Time is precious, and if you're not buying their product, someone else will. Salesmen also don't get paid by the hour like coaches and therapists, nor do they get kickbacks for creating more clients.

They want to make a quick sale and move on, period.

If you already have a chip on your shoulder, you might take a more confrontational approach. You might even make a sarcastic response to their sales pitch. Salesmen really don't like sarcasm. It makes them feel inferior, not in control. I'm not saying you shouldn't use sarcasm – I've used it once or twice myself – just warning you that you're not going to receive any pretend sympathy if you go in this direction.

However you decide to indicate that you've heard it all before and need a better sales pitch, it won't make much of a difference in terms of the outcome. The salesmen are going to respond in one of three ways:

1) Give up immediately. The conversation might go something like this:

> SALESMAN: I have a girl for you. She's pretty and sweet. Do you want her number?
> YOU: Well, you haven't really told me much.
> SALESMAN: I guess you're not interested. Oh well. Good luck.

Don't forget to thank him for trying.

2) Push harder. They will pretend to listen to you and take your concerns seriously, for a time, but this is only to win your trust. Remember at all times that the purpose of this conversation is to convince you to say yes. Even if this person truly cares about you, that is their goal. That is the only outcome that will make them happy.

Even people who care can be very selfish that way.

3) Turn against you. You have frustrated the salesman. You have dashed his hopes for a quick sale and jeopardized his hopes for any sale at all. You have bruised his ego. Worst of all, you're just a single. Singles are supposed to be grateful and agreeable. You put up resistance, and now you're going to pay for it.

The salesman will drop any pretense of being your advocate. Oh, he will still try to help you – by now trying to sell you on the idea that you are a foolish, self-defeating, unmarriageable loser who needs to find someone who can *really* help you.

This is why you aren't married, you will inevitably be told by a jilted salesman. You can't expect me to know everything about a girl. I can't tell you she's the right one. You have to take a chance and meet her instead of asking so many questions. You have to learn to trust people. You don't really want to get married. And, of course, you're too picky.

When the sour grape finally finishes dripping vinegar, he

might even slander you to other bitter salesmen, who love to compile lists of singles, trade in them, and gossip about them. This will all be done for a constructive purpose, of course, since his friends shouldn't waste their time trying to fix you up, either. Even though he ostensibly wants someone to "help" you, he will take perverse pleasure in watching you remain single, and even spoiling you in the eyes of others. You said no, and you even had the nerve to question his sales pitch. Clearly, you are the one with the problem here.

Frankly, it takes a lot of nerve to call a single one vaguely knows and launch into a sales pitch. How presumptuous for someone to suggest a life partner for a person with whom he has never even had a deep conversation! Some people even cold call someone they never met and launch into a sales pitch – without any interest in meeting the person or spending any reasonable time getting to know him.

Sure, it's worked before. Monkeys throwing darts have beaten the stock market, too. That doesn't make it a good idea.

A salesman has merchandise they are trying to sell, and they are looking for buyers. They are not trying to determine what is in your best interests as a customer, but which product they can most likely sell you. If they don't have a product that is right for you, they will go up and down their inventory looking for one that is close enough to offer a potential sale. Again, it's not about you.

Someone who is prioritizing *your* feelings and best interests will first spend a great deal of time getting to know you, your specific needs and desires, and the manner in which you are comfortable being introduced to a potential date. They will earn your confidence by listening to you, being honest with you, and working with you on your terms. After all, it's your personal life. You should decide who you let in and under what terms. Only *then* will be they begin to think of possible matches. Furthermore, they will not be put off by your feedback. They will welcome it! After all, good feedback will help them fine-tune their efforts to help you. A good salesman is customer-centric!

They might not make a suggestion after all, and that's fine too. This jewel of a person will only suggest someone if they have a meaningful basis for doing so. The used car salesman first thinks of the merchandise he is looking to move, then tries to finagle a sale. Someone who does it the right way thinks about you first, then considers the possibilities. They don't urge to go out with whatever is behind door number two, and they definitely don't try to talk you into something that doesn't resonate.

If you are single, don't be afraid to stand up for yourself to used car salesmen pushing you, pressuring you, or making inappropriate personal comments about you. The worst thing that can happen is that they will decide never to try to sell you something again. Insert your own sarcastic comment here for practice.

People who do this – and there are a lot of them – actually think they are being wonderfully kind and thoughtful by calling someone they barely know and suggesting a life partner. In reality this is a selfish act. This clumsy attempt to "help" another person is really about them. They may be anticipating a sizable reward for making a substantial introduction. Some people believe if they make a certain number of successful matches they get a free pass to heaven (apparently regardless of how much carnage they cause in the process). If nothing else, the "benefactor" gets to feel good about himself and forever boast of his successful matchmaking.

Don't kid yourself; as counter-intuitive as it seems, the motivation for many people to perform acts of kindness has more to do with what they get out of it than the actual kindness. Of course it is better for people to help others for ulterior motives than not to help at all, but if they are oblivious to the sensitivities of their pet charity case they may cause more harm than good. That free pass might confer entrance to a different terminus.

If it is really about you, the person calling will be patient, sensitive, non-judgmental, and actually listen. Give that person your greatest respect. If it is clear that it is not about you, don't feel you owe them anything or need them for anything.

If you are married (or a matchmaking single), please, don't insinuate yourself into the personal life of another person unless you are prepared to do it right. Instead of acting like a used car salesman, try being more like a personal shopper.

Whatever you do, don't be like a monkey trying to beat the stock market.

Chapter 6
How low will you go?

Another telltale sign that you've become an "older" single is when would-be matchmakers routinely preface their sales pitch with "Would you be willing to..."

Generally speaking it is bad manners to interrupt someone. This is one exception. Cut them off right then and there and say, "No, I wouldn't." Trust me on this.

If you don't react quickly enough, you will find yourself in the center of a Middle Eastern bazaar, with your dignity the commodity under negotiation. Would you be willing to date someone who is divorced? What if she has kids? What if she's a widow? Would you be willing to date someone a little over-weight? (Really, it's just a little, you'd hardly even notice.) What if she's a little more than a little overweight but she's working on it? Would you be willing to date someone who lives in a faraway place? Would you be willing to date someone with a minor handicap? What about a major handicap?

What in the world are you supposed to answer to any of these questions? If you are too dismissive, you will be con-demned for being judgmental and closed-minded, and a cat-alog of whatever is "less than ideal" about you will be sure to follow. How's that for starting things off on the right foot?

On the other hand, if you leave the door open a crack, this person is going to try to see just how wide he can force it open. If you're willing to date someone with burns on seventy percent on her body, what about eighty percent? What's another ten percent in the grand scheme of things? Marriage is forever. Don't be so closed-minded.

Instead of having a conversation about what you want and need in a partner, the conversation will center around what you're willing to settle for and why you're not willing to settle for more. There is no way this can turn out well for you. If you agree to be fixed up with the person, it will be almost impossi-ble not to obsess over the dreaded "problem", and if you reject the idea you'll feel like a judgmental jerk.

It's easy to understand why matchmakers begin the con-versation this way. They're covering themselves. If they don't mention the "problem" at all, they are gambling that you will be so enamored with the person that you won't hold it against them for concealing the information. That's one in a million. Believe it or not, some matchmakers have such hubris that they play this game time and time again without compunction. In their mind, the one time it works out more than makes up for all the times it doesn't, and proves they know better, too. Beware of such people. They are out there, and they know someone perfect for you.

Even if a matchmaker first extols the virtues of your potential date and then tries to slip in the fine print later on, you'll probably be annoyed that they didn't mention it sooner. So from the matchmaker's perspective, they often feel compelled to mention the caveat immediately just to get it out of the way and protect themselves.

The problem is that this puts you in a no-win situation. You're being asked to decide, without any other information, whether in principle you would be willing to consider someone with a particular "drawback". It's not as if you get to choose between two people who are exactly the same and one has a complication. You're being asked to decide if you would ever be willing to consider someone who has a particular complication, without knowing anything else about the person. Why would you say yes? But how could you say no?

The only other possible response is "it depends". While this is reasonable, it will be taken by the matchmaker as a yes. Now they've pinned you down. You're open to people with "issues". They know more people with "issues" than people who are open to dating them. So now that's what you're going to get. There's no going back, either. Once you get whittled down in a negotiation, you don't get a do-over. Your last concession becomes the new starting point.

What we have here are conflicting needs between all concerned parties. Some matchmakers really mean well and want to be up front with singles (and cover themselves, too). Singles should be able to make informed decisions without being accused of being soulless narcissists. Singles who have baggage or complications should also be given a fair chance in dating, without being rejected out of hand. So how can we make things fair for everyone?

There is no perfect solution here. The best option is for people to meet naturally, where they can get to know each other without any pressure. When this happens, it will be much easier for people to appreciate others' qualities and gently absorb whatever is complicated, in the proper context. When you meet a real human being before actually dating them, you will find that some factors you didn't think about matter a great deal, and other items that you thought were deal-breakers are really not so important after all.

When you're already in date-mode, this process of discovery is scary and threatening. Instead of learning something about a person and processing it, the natural reaction is to think about whether you can live with that for the rest of your life, and why you should even bother trying.

When it comes to introducing people, the best approach is not to have a negotiating session at all. Drop that idea completely. Simply tell singles about another person openly and honestly, and let them make a decision. It is inevitable that the "drawbacks" will weigh heavily on their scales, and it is also inevitable that singles will imagine whatever you tell them about a person to be worse than it actually is. You can discuss this with them, but respect whatever they decide. They have more right to judge who they date than you have to judge their decisions.

In a perfect world, no one would be superficial or closed-minded, singles would be thought of as human beings and not commodities with price tags, and dating in general would be pleasant and exciting. The world might never be perfect, but we can certainly do a lot better. One small step in that direction is to cut out the negotiation sessions.

Singles, insist on that being part of the deal.

Chapter 7
The age of desperation

It happens around the time when you are no longer just another person, but a Single. The exact age varies widely between societies, but every society that places serious value on marriage has one. It is the age of desperation.

Religious and close-knit communities tend to have traditional structures for getting their young people married. This almost invariably includes formal introductions by community members or recognized matchmakers. Some communities also provide social outlets where young people can meet and form relationships, but many religious communities have strict guidelines for such interactions to prevent unseemly behavior. Such places by definition rely almost exclusively on matchmaking to marry off their children.

Other types of communities, such as large metro centers and non-sectarian college campuses, are the complete opposite. In these environments singles rely almost entirely on social events and friends to meet people for possible relationships. Formal matchmaking might be available as well, but generally it is viewed as an anachronism or a novelty at best.

Despite the polar dissimilarity between these two types of communities, they share one fascinating thing in common. Once singles reach the age of desperation – whether it's 20, 45, or anything in between – they will be encouraged to do that which until then had been frowned upon. Religious communities that consider fraternization of the sexes to be taboo will encourage "older" singles to attend singles events. (Even if these events are "supervised" by religious proxies, a singles event of any kind is seen as a major concession. It is an emergency measure that they would be thrilled to abolish.) Conversely, communities that rely on socialization will encourage those who are unsuccessful to try matchmaking. Indeed, there are many matchmaking services for "single professionals", and they cater almost exclusively to a mature crowd.

Several interesting points emerge from this phenomenon. First, most people begin dating with a pre-programmed set of expectations for how they will get married, falling into the classic trap of believing there is a formula for meeting the right one. Because of this, they will close themselves off to perfectly reasonable alternatives for meeting people. If an opportunity presents itself that is somewhat unconventional, young singles will often reject the opportunity solely on that basis. They are more concerned about what their friends will think than the consequences of turning down a good opportunity. Young people think they are invincible, and young singles think they will always have better opportunities than the one they just passed up. Doing something "weird" that smacks of loserdom just isn't worth it when you only live in the present.

I'm going to share with you a startling revelation. No one is born into this world as an older single. Every older single was once a younger single. Young singles who are cavalier about rejecting quality suitors and turning down opportunities because they are a little out of their comfort zone have an excellent chance of becoming older singles. By the time they realize they are not everyone's greatest desire and those good opportunities begin to dry up, it might already be too late. The best opportunity one will ever have might well be the one he squanders early on. The how-to guide for not getting married is facetious, but it's no joke.

Second, most people are willing to veer from their pre-programmed script only through desperation. The more desperate they become, the more willing they will be to try different things. While this is understandable, it reflects a lack of wisdom. The various methods of meeting all have pros and cons, and different methods work better for different people. The goal is to facilitate one's path to a successful marriage, not to validate the expectations of one's surroundings.

If social events have something to offer strictly religious singles, they should be available from day one, not only as a last resort. If formal matchmaking can help even social butterflies, there should be no stigma attached to it. Waiting until you are desperate to venture out of your comfort zone will only compound the feeling of desperation and loserdom, which doesn't help singles make smart decisions or make them more attractive to others. Far better to just do whatever you think can work, right away, and don't look back. If people look at you funny for trying something a little out of the box, you and your spouse will have a good laugh about it later on.

Third, societies tend to be much more concerned with perpetuating their social mores than serving the needs of their members. There is something fundamentally immoral about this – and I say this as someone who believes very strongly in tradition. Societies need to learn how to balance their traditions with the needs of the individual. Not everyone who has a slightly different need should be viewed as someone with a problem, let alone a mortal threat to the entire society. Lest the non-religious think they are superior, everywhere you go they have created cliques, clubs, and caste systems that marginalize those who don't conform, even as they pay lip service to individuality. It's okay to be a little different as long as you're basically like everyone else.

It's ironic that the first choice of one society is the last resort of the other; those who insist on matchmaking early on will attend singles events when they become desperate, and vice versa. As time goes on, and singles become increasingly desperate, the revised script will be more practical and goal-based regardless of the society of origin: do whatever might work for you.

Wouldn't it be better to make this the game plan for everyone from day one?

Chapter 8
Artificial substitutes

If you remain single after your years in school, your opportunities to meet someone naturally and get to know them gradually plummet forever. This is a bigger problem than you might realize, because there is no better way to meet a potential spouse. Matchmaking, singles events, and online dating all work some of the time, as anything will, but all of these methods of meeting are contrived, awkward, and less effective.

Consider the following. When singles who never met before share a ride to a singles event, they will naturally talk during the ride. The conversation is likely to be free-flowing and relaxed, even if they have little in common and no attraction to one another. If they discover they *do* have significant things in common and good "chemistry", they will probably decide to see each other again.

If these same two people met for the first time at the actual event, the conversation would likely be contrived, formulaic, and awkward. They are far less likely to discover that they have significant things in common, and unless there is strong physical attraction there will be no "chemistry". Needless to say, the odds of them deciding to go out will be very low.

Think about this. Both scenarios are really just two people meeting for the first time, introducing themselves to one another, and having a conversation. One might think that the outcome should therefore be exactly the same. Either they will have that indefinable "spark", or they will not…right?

Wrong. It is not enough merely for two people to meet. The context in which they meet is absolutely critical to their chances of enjoying each other's company, then naturally deciding that they would like to spend more time together. It's true that if you boil down both scenarios to their very essence, it is two people meeting and having a basic conversation. However, in the first scenario it is entirely natural for them to be having this conversation. They both have a reason for being in each other's company independent of the fact that they are single and looking. They both need to get to the event, and they are happy to share a ride whether or not there is romantic potential. Hence, there is a pretext for them to talk, and it will be devoid of pressure, awkwardness, and expectations.

If they meet instead at the singles event, there is no reason for them to talk except to determine if there is romantic potential. If they could intuit that there was no possibility for romance, they would not waste each other's time when they could be meeting someone else. Therefore, when they do talk at the event, it is really just a thinly veiled pre-date interview. This is anything but fun, and is less likely to bring out the best sides of each other's personalities. Instead of being their natural selves, they will be in "date mode", with its accompanying shields and screening process.

These two people might in reality be right for one another, but since they are meeting in a contrived and uncomfortable context, they will never discover that potential. Ironically, singles have a better chance of connecting before and after a singles event than during the event itself!

To make matters worse, events create a terrible dilemma for singles. You don't really have a chance to get to know people, and you have to make serious judgments based on very little information. After perhaps a snatch of conversation – which may be entirely superficial – you have to decide very quickly if you will take the plunge and ask the person out, or risk never seeing her again. There is usually no middle ground.

Married people will scoff at this dilemma. They will encourage singles to always take the plunge, arguing that they have nothing to lose. This is arrogant and shortsighted. Asking someone out after a snatch of conversation doesn't work out in real life the way it does in the movies. Transitioning from a brief introduction to an actual date is a giant leap that is bold, but not really romantic. These two people don't really know one another, and it is not natural for them to be dating. It is forced, since there is no middle ground. Either they date or they part ways forever (unless they happen to meet at another event).

You might be bold in these situations, but reality will force you to be gun-shy. You will be inexplicably turned down for dates by people who seemed to enjoy your company. Some people will actually look distressed when you ask them out, which will do wonders for your confidence. Sometimes they will agree to go out, but you will discover very quickly that you are not compatible, and you might wind up in a very uncomfortable situation. This will provide negative reinforcement the next time you have a pleasant snatch of conversation with a stranger.

Ideally, singles should be able to get to know one another gradually and develop a mutual interest that will naturally transition to dating. This process is pleasant and enjoyable, and they will be excited to go out. Older singles have few such opportunities.

I strongly encourage communities to create more opportunities for singles to get to know one another gradually, in situations where the conversations have a natural pretext. Ongoing programs, volunteer work, and educational forums all provide opportunities for people with shared interests to meet in a low-pressure environment. The conversations will flow more freely, and the best sides of people's personalities will have a chance to shine. This will allow singles to develop interest in one another for meaningful reasons that will make a transition to dating more likely and more enjoyable.

I also strongly encourage singles to look for these opportunities, to take full advantage of them, and to create these opportunities themselves if their community fails to do so. Many singles – particularly women – flock to singles event after singles event because "everyone is there for one reason", while they shun natural meeting opportunities. This is a big mistake. Singles events are all about "getting right down to business", but a room full of people in "date mode" is not conducive to pleasant interactions. Counter-intuitive as it might seem, non-singles events provide a much better meeting opportunity, precisely because advertising that one is single and desperate is not a prerequisite for attending.

Remember, the people who meet in a carpool to an event have a much better chance of dating than the people who meet at the event itself. Natural is always better than artificial.

Chapter 9
Fail to succeed

You don't need to be single to encounter warped thinking, but it definitely helps. Most people can fake being rational and sensible most of the time. When it comes to dating, that goes right out the window. There are few areas of life in which people exhibit their true inner nuttiness quite so readily.

As we've discussed at length, if you remain single past a certain age many people will automatically assume that there is something wrong with you or your methods. There is one surprising exception to this – a man who gets married and then divorced.

This might sound counter-intuitive, but many women would rather date a man who is divorced than one who was never married at all. In their eyes, a divorced man has proven his quality. He managed to convince at least one woman in this universe to go for him. The fact that the marriage went up in flames is secondary to the fact that he managed to get married in the first place. Young single men might be surprised to learn that many women think this way, but it's true. If you're going to be single after a certain age, it's a distinct advantage to have a failed marriage under your belt.

The same bizarre mentality does not apply in the other direction. Men generally have a strong preference for a woman who was never married, and view with suspicion a woman who has been divorced. Is she a home-wrecker? Is she impossible to please? Will she drive him crazy, then take off with half his money? The fact that she convinced another man to commit to her will not work in her favor.

This bias against single men who have never been married is a cruel twist. It is bad enough that married people wonder what is wrong with them that they never got married. It is bad enough that single women wonder the same thing. Then they learn that every jerk who ruined a woman's life has a better chance of getting remarried than they have of getting married at all. A divorcee gets the benefit of the doubt; the never-married man is guilty until proven innocent.

But this myopic thinking goes even further. Women are leery of men who have not dated anyone in a while. They are assumed to be losers. On the one hand they don't want a "player" who is always dating someone new, but at least a "player" is attractive to many women. Someone with sincere intentions who is waiting for the real deal is also guilty until proven innocent.

Women also want to find assurance in knowing that a man has had long-term relationships. Obviously all such relationships have failed, but the mere fact that he kept a woman in his life for an extended period of time raises his value in the eyes of other women. Better to fail spectacularly, break a woman's heart to pieces, string someone along for months or years, or otherwise take a long time to realize this isn't meant to be than to break up sooner without lots of collateral damage. The former presumably demonstrates that one can "almost" make it work; maybe a slight adjustment in his swing will turn him into a home-run hitter. The latter is evidence of a singles hitter with questionable ability.

If you want to succeed in dating, it helps to have at least a few spectacular failures along the way. Women will appreciate you for it.

Chapter 10
Child's play

In the good old days, children became contributing members of society from a very early age. They did work on the farm, errands in the home, and helped out in the store. They had to. They were another mouth to feed, and everyone had to pull their own weight. Poverty isn't fun, but it sure helps one develop a strong work ethic.

Nowadays, adolescence typically extends far into adulthood, and for some it continues indefinitely. Young adults take many years to "find themselves", carry a strong sense of entitlement, learn nothing from history, scorn their predecessors, live only in the moment, and abhor responsibilities (other than that they're better than ever). No wonder they marry later and remain married shorter; marriage runs counter to all of the above. No wonder they would rather have a pet than reproduce; the next generation spells their own obsolescence.

For some reason, whenever someone says to an assembly of young people "You are the future", everyone in the room applauds. People sure are suckers.

Sometimes extended adolescence is not by choice, but imposed upon a person by his society. Many people view singles as children and treat them accordingly - irrespective of their maturity level or accomplishments. This is reflected in several ways:

1) People naturally assume that children do not know what is best for them. They assume quite the same about singles.

2) People generally do not respect the opinions of children, let

alone solicit them. Singles can provide valuable feedback about the realities of dating, but their status renders their thoughts irrelevant in the eyes of many. Someone who gets married at eighteen is assumed to know more about dating and relationships than someone who has been through the ringer for many years without being fortunate enough to marry. A single might not be one's first destination for advice on raising children (though anyone can have valuable insight), but surely he is more in touch with what's wrong with the world of dating and how it can be improved than someone who never really experienced it.

True story. One time I was fixed up with a girl and noticed that she seemed to disconnect from the date after about fifteen minutes. My suspicions were later confirmed, and I learned the reason. She had asked what I like to do in my spare time. I mentioned that I write. She asked what I write, and I told her that I have written several books. She asked what they were about, and I told her a little about each of them. One of my books discusses what is wrong with the world of dating specifically in the Orthodox Jewish community and what needs to be done to fix it. She found it highly offensive that a single would lecture others on this subject, and wrote me off right then and there.

This is absurd. First of all, she made a negative judgment about me without having even read the book (which is far more presumptuous than writing about something with which one has a great deal of experience). Second of all, even if it were true that I was a personal failure, that didn't mean my perspective and ideas were invalid. The world is full of coaches who can't play, editors who can't write, doctors who smoke, dietitians who take poor care of themselves, and numerous others who dispense advice to others that they fail to put into practice. We're all more or less okay with that. We recognize that someone can give expert opinions while being demonstrably imperfect in his own life.

The greatest exception to this (with flawed religious leaders a distant second) is singles who claim to know a thing or two about dating and relationships. Married people have no tolerance for such a person. Some married people go so far as to urge singles to seek advice only from those who are married (the actual health of the marriage is not considered).

This young lady clearly drank that cup of Kool-Aid down to the last drop.

On an unrelated note, she worked as a doula, despite having never experienced pregnancy and childbirth personally.

You can't make this stuff up.

3) People generally do not worry about a child being embarrassed in public. If they feel the need to rebuke a child, they will do so in the presence of others without a second thought. I'm not justifying this behavior, merely noting that it is not viewed as a terrible social misstep. Conversely, society expects one to rebuke an adult discreetly; the crime of embarrassing him in public will almost always be viewed as more severe than whatever the person did to deserve it. Similarly, people have few compunctions about discussing something very personal in the child's life in the presence of others, which is not at all acceptable when it comes to adults.

Not so when it comes to singles. They get the kid's meal here too. As a single you can expect people to ask you about your personal life in social settings, and even discuss fixing you up with someone while many bystanders are only too glad to eavesdrop. Those same people would likely show more tact if the subject of conversation concerned other personal matters, such as medical issues or one's financial situation. When it comes to your status as a single, your personal life is an open book for all to probe whenever and wherever it is convenient for them. Discretion simply does not exist.

If you protest their public invasion of your personal life, they will rebuke you. You should be grateful that they are thinking of you, period. Children do not have the privilege of establishing boundaries and ground rules; neither do you.

4) If you express reservations about being fixed up by some-one who doesn't seem to have a good handle on things, they might have a delightful suggestion. Arrange to visit them at home some time and the young lady they have in mind for you will just happen to be there as well. You'll be able to meet her without the pressure and awkwardness of a blind date.

How fun! Not only will you be able to make stilted small talk with the young lady under the leering supervision of this amateur matchmaker, surely she will have absolutely no inkling that your being there is anything more than a pure coincidence. Under no circumstances will anyone in the room have any hopes or expectations that this "chance" meeting will lead to an actual date. Or course not!

Parents arrange play dates for children. Married people arrange play dates for singles. Unfortunately, only the children are likely to enjoy the experience.

5) Children love to play silly games. Since singles are still con-sidered children, adults who arrange events for singles make sure to include lots of silly games. This is intended to lighten the atmosphere and facilitate natural meetings. What could be more fun and natural than a bunch of educated, professional, accomplished men and women playing games you might find at a birthday party for pre-teens?

If you protest that these activities are contrived and degrad-ing, the married adult in charge will turn into the principal from hell faster than Superman changing in a phone booth. Married adults don't like smart talk from singles. Singles are supposed to do what they are told and pretend to enjoy it. Otherwise they deserve to be single and miserable forever.

Married adults also believe that enjoyable activities should have the natural fun sucked out of them and replaced with artificial, controlled fun. If married people do not control the fun, they cannot take credit for the fun, and that makes it harder for them to take credit if singles meet. Married people desperately want to be able to take credit, and will crush anyone who challenges how they control events. Thank God for small favors; at least these people are running singles events and not countries.

One time a friend told me about a bowling event with pizza. This sounded like a rare event for singles, as opposed to a singles event (as discussed in Chapter 8). I enjoy bowling and pizza, so I decided to attend on that basis. The possibility of meeting my future spouse was entirely tangential. This allowed me to approach the event without any feeling of pressure or discomfort. I could truly "be myself". If I enjoyed the company as well, that would be a bonus. If not, it wouldn't really matter. I was there for the bowling and pizza, not the wistful hope of meeting my soul mate.

I arrived on time, which naturally meant I was quite early, and introduced myself to the organizer. We had a pleasant chat, during which I related my own efforts to encourage more natural meeting opportunities for singles and expressed appreciation for her doing the same.

It was all downhill from there.

After more people arrived and groups formed for bowling, the organizer announced that we would not be bowling normally. Instead, the men would all bowl a single frame at their respective lanes, then move to the next lane. They would continue this game of musical chairs after each frame. The women would remain at their respective lanes during this bizarre affair.

I took the organizer aside and suggested that it would make more sense to let each group remain together for a complete game, then shuffle the groups for a second game. Granted, not everyone would meet everyone else, but there was no reason to force it. Far better to spend significant time getting to know a few people than a snatch of time hardly getting to know anyone at all.

Besides, why not allow everyone to enjoy a real game of bowling? Why turn it into a speed dating event? If the purpose of the event was strictly to have forced meetings, and the bowling was a sham, better to dispense with the bowling altogether and have real speed dating. No need for subterfuge. If, however, the purpose was to let people meet naturally, then leave them alone and let them bowl normally. (Also, if she insisted on having players rotate during the game, the women should be the ones changing lanes, since they cared less about bowling anyway.)

The organizer, playing God as she was, dismissed my suggestions. She said if I didn't like it I could leave. Afterward, she sent me a deranged email in which she made a series of nasty personal comments, such as that the women at the event were unhappy that I attended, I was of poor appearance, and that for me to get married I needed to meet as many women as possible, to increase the chance that one would overlook all my unattractive qualities. How nice.

A great many people who involve themselves with singles – be they matchmakers, event organizers, or typical armchair quarterbacks trying to "help" – will have this sort of visceral reaction toward singles who question their methods. This is not merely a knee-jerk response to criticism, since married people who offer the same input will be treated with more respect and patience. Singles are expected to shut up and do what they are told. Perhaps psychologists can conduct a study to determine why so many people who hold singles in low-esteem – often even in contempt – try to "help" them in the first place. It seems their efforts are more self-serving in essence than altruistic.

The point here (aside from sharing an interesting story) is that singles are once again treated like children. They could be highly successful and respected in their daily lives, but singles events are time machines that transport them back to kindergarten. Children who question how the teacher runs the classroom will generally be disciplined – even if they are respectful, and even if they are right. Only adults are allowed to give their feedback. Singles who question a matchmaker or event organizer will be similarly punished. Only married adults are allowed to suggest how singles should be controlled.

While I certainly blame those who infantilize singles, I blame singles as well for submitting to this degradation. God decides our fortunes, not some arrogant gatekeeper, and God does not expect singles to degrade themselves in order to get dates. Those who truly believe that God runs the world will avail themselves of human assistance, since that is the natural order of the world, but will not allow others to rob them of their basic dignity for so cheap a price as admission to a singles event or a blind date. Those who reject the idea of a real God inevitably appoint others in His stead, though it is not clear to what advantage.

Even if we leave God completely out of the equation (which I don't think can or should be done), there is no reason for singles to accept maltreatment by married peers who view themselves as superior. I was not the only person at the bowling event who thought the speed dating was silly and unnecessary – but I was the only one with the courage to say something about it. If even a few people requested for groups to bowl an entire game together, I'm sure the organizer would have smiled and relented. Who knows, perhaps one or two matches might have resulted that were otherwise hindered. Rolling a ball and then running to another lane is not a likely catalyst for a romantic connection.

Singles, you must take greater responsibility for how you allow others to treat you. Don't expect people to treat you any better than you treat yourself. If a singles event is organized in a way that reflects condescension toward singles, you owe it to yourself to say something, even if they don't listen. If a matchmaker asks inappropriate and intrusive questions, or makes degrading personal remarks, you shouldn't take it silently. These are not tyrants who hold your life in the balance, and you don't need to kiss their ring. They are just misguided married people at best, in which case you should help educate them, or nasty married people at worst, in which case they shouldn't be involved with singles at all.

The worst thing that can happen is that they will say some

nasty personal things, like the organizer did to me, and then leave your life forever. This mean, small-minded person who has no respect for you will no longer try to help you get married.

No great loss.

Chapter 11
Awkward moments

For many singles, dating provides a steady stream of awkward moments. The following situations will happen regularly:

1) You will be on a date with someone and realize very quickly that there is no possible way you will ever have a serious relationship with the person. There is no convenient eject button that comes with this realization, nor is there any polite way you can excuse yourself. You have to see the date through, and you have to be pleasant company. At the same time, you don't want to be the most likable version of yourself, lest your date enjoy your company too much, think you are having the time of your life, and be hurt to learn you don't want to see her again. Basically, you have to be a little bit of a jerk, without being too much of a jerk. If you aren't a little bit of a jerk, then you're the worst sort of jerk. There's no way out. Every disease known to man will be cured before a solution is found to this problem.

2) You will be on a date with someone and realize very quickly that she is not very interested in you. She is trying to be polite but is not doing a convincing job. If you try even harder to make her like you, you will only make her more uncomfortable and possibly even force her to short-circuit the date. If you try to give her a free escape by acknowledging that things don't seem to be working out, you will make her feel guilty, and might even come across as a jerk for putting her on the spot. Once again, the only thing you can do is stick it out and absorb some awkward moments. Drink your coffee more quickly. It is

generally acceptable to end a date after the coffee is finished. Just don't guzzle it.

3) You will go out with a girl and you will think she is a lovely person, but only on the inside. Unfortunately, you are unable to recognize her exterior beauty as well, much as you would like to. Being the lovely person that she is, she actually likes you and would be interested in pursuing a relationship with you that would be full of love, devotion, and mutual respect. You'd like that – you really would – but it's just not going to happen. You're not even remotely attracted to her. You never will be. No shot. You're going to need to end it, it's unfair to string her along, and you can't let on in the slightest way that her appearance has anything to do with it. In reality her appearance is the *only* thing that has anything to do with it. Even though you know this is reasonable and that you're not a superficial sleazeball, you still feel like one.

4) You will experience the following as a blind date approaches you: *That's definitely not her. It can't be her. Wait a minute, could that be her? I sure hope not! Please, God, don't let it be her. Oh no…* Then you will smile and say, "Hi! Nice to meet you."

Of course this date is over even before it starts, which is even worse than the previous scenarios. At least in those cases you can be into the date for at least a short time. In this case you will be faking it from the very beginning, hating yourself and pitying yourself every agonizing moment. You know it's not fair for her, but, honestly, it's really not fair for you either. Hell could conceivably resemble something like this.

In some cases you will even be embarrassed to be seen in public with the person. When this happens you might briefly consider whether there is any possibility you can excuse yourself from the date, pretend to be someone else, or simply run away. Don't bother; you cannot do any of these things. There is no way out.

You will try to think of where you can go that keeps your

chances of being seen by anyone you know to an absolute minimum. You will then try to think of the best way to get there that does the same.

The older you get as a single, the more often this will happen to you. There are several reasons for this:

Attractive people are more likely to leave the pool of singles as time goes on. As you age, there will be increasingly fewer attractive people remaining, and you will be fixed up with whatever is left.

People who remain single a long time are more likely to let themselves go at some point, and you will meet them after that point.

The older you get, a higher percentage of your dates are likely to be blind dates. If you meet someone naturally, physical attraction will be an issue zero percent of the time. After all, you saw each other first and decided to go out. If you're fixed up with someone, how they look is the main concern you will have before meeting. Those fears are going to be well-founded much of the time, and with increasing frequency as time goes on.

5) If you go out with a person even one time, you are forever linked. For the entire rest of you life, every time you cross paths you must exchange awkward pleasantries. If you are at a social gathering with a thousand other people and are at opposite ends of the room, you must wade through the crowd just to say hello, ask her how she is doing, tell her you're doing fine as well, and it's good to see her. That's the law. If you pretend not to see her or otherwise don't go through these obligatory motions, you are an insensitive person who is embarrassing her.

Stay single long enough and every social event will be a ghoulish reunion with numerous people you would rather forget. You will make the rounds saying hello to everyone you went out with previously, then try to avoid them all. If you get married and divorced and never speak to your ex again, people will understand. If you merely go out with someone and fail to exchange pleasantries, no punishment is too small for you.

Marriage may well be temporary. Awkward pleasantries are forever.

6) Married people will make clumsy attempts to fix you up. To their great surprise and consternation, these attempts will be unsuccessful. Some of these married people will then cease speaking to you for no clear reason, and will forever be uncomfortable in your presence. Whereas you must acknowledge every person you ever went out with every time you see them, married people who fix you up haphazardly don't ever have to acknowledge you again. You don't like it? Get married. In the mean time, get used to people averting their gaze from you with the same lack of grace they employed in suggesting a soul mate.

7) The following scenario might be the most awkward of them all. Someone will approach you and try to fix you up with their single daughter, granddaughter, sister, niece, etc. If the person seems cool you will probably perk up; they are not trying to fix you up with a random stranger but someone they know and care about. If they don't seem like someone you want for an in-law, you will already feel awkward. Either way, it's going to get a lot worse. They will tell you how stunning the young lady is, and they will just happen to have a picture of her to prove it. They will excitedly foist this picture upon you. No matter how much you protest, they will insist that you look at it, convinced that you will be overwhelmed by her beauty and consent to the introduction forthwith.

The moment when you gaze at the picture will be worse than a kick to the stomach. There is no way you can say that you are turned off by what you see, the apple of his eye. You certainly cannot suggest that the young lady apply for her own zip code. You will try to keep a poker face while you are panicking, desperately searching for the right words to escape the situation. The only thing you know at this moment is that there is no way you are going out with this girl. The picture-wielding matchmaker will be leering at you with a goofy smile on his face, completely misreading your dumbfounded reaction. This is one of those agonizing situations where the truth will not work, but there is no white lie that will bail you out. Once you have seen the picture, it's all about the picture.

You will finally mumble something about her being very pretty but not quite your type, while this well-meaning relative of the girl becomes crestfallen before your eyes, then proudly defiant. The next moment you will be left standing there, trying to articulate an apology to the back he has turned to you, while you wonder why he is the victim who deserves an apology.

How did you even get into this mess? You were just minding your own business. Some guy showed you a picture of a girl you don't want to marry, and now you're a shallow, insensitive fool. How you will ever face this person again? Should you move? What if you move and it happens again?

You will be forced to listen to many clumsy sales pitches, but a picture really is worth a thousand words. No words, however, will get you out of this situation unscathed.

8) You will be on a first or second date and she will bump into a friend. Is this a coincidence, or did she plan the "accidental" encounter so her friend could check you out? Even if it is the former, her friend will be checking you out and discussing it with her later, so now you're performing for an audience. The girl will also be conscious of what her friend thinks. Most likely she is not especially proud to be in your company, and her enthusiasm for your company will not increase after this awkward moment. Once something unpleasant happens on a date it tends to be a downward spiral.

Does she introduce you to her friend or not? It's going to be awkward either way, since it's challenging enough to make conversation with the person you are already on a date with and hardly know. You certainly don't need the additional burden of making friendly chit-chat with her friend. At the same time, your date will be evaluating your performance during this bizarre interruption to the regularly scheduled programming.

How well do you roll with the unexpected? How well can she see you getting along with her friends? How impressive are you? You have nothing to say and no way to say it, but you have to deliver some majestic banter or you're finished.

If she doesn't introduce you to her friend, then she is probably hinting to her friend that she got stuck on a date with you and doesn't plan on seeing you again. If she does introduce you to her friend, but by name only, she is leaving it to you to make things less awkward for herself. If she introduces you *as* a friend, she is only being polite, since you hardly know each other and might never see each other again after this date. If she says anything that makes you feel at ease with yourself and the situation, you might want to propose right then and there.

If she spends more than ten seconds chit-chatting with her friend while you sit there awkwardly, your place on the totem pole should be abundantly clear. If you whipped out your phone and sent a quick text to a friend just to make a point, I would disagree with your approach and admire it at the same time.

If you are the one to bump into a friend, it will be no less awkward and challenging. A good friend will size up the situation and simply leave you alone. Oftentimes it will just be an acquaintance, someone without any social graces who will be excited and curious to see you on a date. This is a good opportunity for you to demonstrate your ability to handle uncomfortable situations, and hopefully your date will be easygoing and impressed.

However, awkwardness tends to highlight the fact that you are on a date with someone you barely know, the whole thing is extremely tenuous, there is a clear separation between the bubble of your date and your real life, and the person you are with doesn't really belong on the other side. All this is entirely reasonable, but once it's brought to the surface by an awkward encounter, it's going to be that much harder to overcome.

Many singles try to reduce the possibility of this happening by meeting in slightly out-of-the-way places for dates. This is sensible, to a point, but some people get carried away with it.

Women in particular tend to be extremely self-conscious about being seen on a date. Ladies, please be subtle and sensitive. If you make too big a deal out of it, the guy will realize that you are embarrassed to be seen with him, which doesn't set a positive tone for a date. Chances are some guys you date won't be proud to be seen in public with you, either, and you will not want them to make that obvious. If a guy takes you out to eat, don't suggest you sit at a table that is walled in from two or three sides. (If you do, then maybe you should insist on paying for the date.)

No matter what you do, every now and then your date will be interrupted with a reminder that you are not really part of each other's lives. It's going to be awkward. Do your best to cut the awkward moment short, be easygoing about it, and appreciate the opportunity to glean something about your date's social graces and her interest in you.

*

These are just some of the more common awkward situations you will encounter. But there will be many others, some of which will be downright weird.

One time my phone rang and a woman on the other end introduced herself with, "Am I disturbing you?" The answer to that depends on who is calling as much as when they are calling, and I had no idea who this person was. After some prodding she actually volunteered her first name. The next thing I knew, this strange woman, who didn't even tell me how she got my number or who she was, tried fixing me up with some girl. By now you can imagine I was less than enthusiastic, but I tried to be polite and open-minded.

The conversation briefly became semi-normal, then turned completely weird. It seems the young lady she had in mind – thirty years of age, no small child – was being represented in this negotiation by her father. After gathering some information about me, the woman said she would speak with him and call me right back.

Remember the leverage bit in the first section of the book? Apparently the other side decided they now had all of it, since the woman called me back with an intrusive question I will not repeat here. My patience finally wore thin, and I gave her a sharp response. She relayed this to the other side, then called me back saying they wanted to know if I wear jeans. This was a thinly veiled test of my "religiosity". I expressed an appropriate degree of outrage and thought it was clear that I had no interest in meeting the self-righteous spinster, but this lady wouldn't give up. She spoke to the other side, then called me back…with yet another question!

This time they wanted to know if my children will join the army (the "right" answer to this question was "of course not"). I told her that I can't possibly say what my unborn children will do when they turn eighteen, but that I would encourage my children to make decisions that are appropriate for them as individuals. This strange lady was shocked by my response, asking if I really believed that a father shouldn't guide his children. I told her that I certainly intended to guide my children, but I also expected them to be different from one another, and anyone who could ask the questions I had been asked was both shallow and stupid. Unfortunately that's not what I was looking for. Call me picky.

One time a man who had never before spoken to me approached me in synagogue and shared that for the last few months he had been praying for me to get married. He wanted to know if my situation had improved during that time.

On the one hand, it's difficult to be furious at someone who is putting in a good word for you with The Boss. On the other hand, a little tact goes a long way.

I responded that dating had actually been worse than usual lately. He looked extremely disappointed – not because of empathy and concern for my personal difficulties, but because his prayers had not borne fruit. Ironically, I tried to encourage *him*, saying that I'm sure every prayer helps.

Then he seemed to remember that he was married and I was single, and this role reversal simply wouldn't do. I needed to do my part too, he smartly noted. Maybe I was missing good opportunities that God was sending me. He seemed convinced that his prayers simply couldn't fail – unless I was failing.

I invited him to read one of my essays on balancing effort and faith, which did not interest him, and we parted ways. He had never spoken to me before, and has not uttered a word to me since, in fact doing the gaze-aversion thing when he sees me.

Because you are single, people will intrude on your personal life completely uninvited, expecting a hero's welcome as they barge in the door to your soul. There is no legal way of eliminating these people, nor a practical way of slamming the door in their face without looking like the bad guy. Society will always support the married person "trying to help" over the single who sets ground rules and boundaries.

Ultimately you can't control how they behave, but you can control how it affects you. It won't take long for you to become preoccupied with avoiding awkward situations. This is a dangerous trap. Part of truly growing up is realizing that life is full of awkward and uncomfortable situations. The trick is not to engineer a strategy that avoids these situations to the point of avoiding life itself, but to develop your ability to transcend these situations when they arise. Trying to avoid awkwardness instead of transcending it only creates greater problems.

There are many examples of this. Simply calling a girl for a date can be awkward, and receiving the call can be just as awkward. Some people deal with this by eliminating this part of the process and relying on a third-party to arrange the first several dates for them. This solution is worse than the problem. Singles who rely on a third-party to this degree stunt their ability to communicate with one another, which is the foundation of any relationship.

Singles are trained by society to lose interest in someone if there is so much as an awkward silence, let alone a conversation that doesn't flow with continuous joyous banter. As soon as things get uncomfortable, run the other way! But bringing a new person into your life is bound to contain some uncomfortable and even tense moments. If a relationship manages to survive the initial few dates, there will surely be questions, doubts, concerns, and fears. Bailing at the first sign of discomfort is one of the rules for not getting married. If you really want to survive as a single, and eventually thrive in a relationship, you need to stop fearing awkwardness. You don't have to enjoy it, but you have to expect it, absorb it, face it head on, and rise above it.

Maybe you will discuss it with the person you are dating and discover that the awkward moment was an opportunity to develop trust and intimacy. Maybe you will both have a good laugh about it and turn the discomfort into a positive experience. Maybe you will find that the worst things you feared might come from the awkward situation were really trivial, and that running away from awkwardness distanced you from something wonderful right behind it.

Awkwardness is really a code word for self-consciousness and fear. People who are truly at ease with themselves do not feel awkward even in unusual situations. Successful and self-confident people always seem to be in control when others feel awkward, earning the admiration of those around them.

Spend less time worrying about awkward situations and the weird behavior of others, and spend more time developing your ability to deal with it. I can't promise that doing so will get you married, but you will be a much better person for it, and this ability will only help you during your single years and beyond.

Chapter 12
Different strokes for married folks

Among the many unpleasant feelings you will experience as you age without a spouse is that you are constantly on trial. Even if you succeed in convincing those around you that you are not sabotaging yourself in dating, that verdict will be appealed over and over again. Every unsuccessful date will be grounds for reopening the trial. The mere passage of time without success will be the same. You can never have the case permanently closed in your favor. The best you can achieve is a stay of execution.

To make matters even more unfair, you don't get to put your accusers on trial. They enjoy a sort of undiplomatic immunity. Whatever you say can and will be used against you, and whatever they say will only be used against you as well.

Here's a prime example. Many of your accusers will take a myopic approach to their prosecution. You have reached a certain age and you are still single. No further information is required. Whatever you did obviously did not work. You need to change and do things their way, or you are guilty. Of course, they are simply railroading you, and attempting to reason with them is like trying to talk a tyrant into stepping down.

But let's say this trial is being conducted within a community where singles are expected to meet one another primarily through matchmaking. In such communities you don't choose who you date; other people choose for you, and all you can do is accept or decline their suggestions. While it's true that your success rate is zero, their success rate (at least with you) is also zero. You can only marry someone you meet, after all, and they are the ones with the most influence over who you actually meet. Unless these matchmakers are wildly successful with other singles – and they are not – why does everyone assume that the problem is with you and your dating practices and not with the people finding you the dates?

Let's put it another way. If you go out with a hundred people and remain single, people will invariably assume that you are too picky and missed some excellent opportunities. They will not even entertain the notion that your soul mate (or a reasonable facsimile thereof) would not be found among such a significant number of people. At the same time, it is highly uncommon to find a matchmaker whose "success rate" is greater than one percent. In other words, for every one hundred matches suggested by the average matchmaker, it is quite likely that fewer than one will result in a marriage. Yet, incredibly, if a matchmaker boasts that they "made" ten matches, everyone will celebrate her as an expert – even if she needed to try a thousand times to achieve those ten matches!

Singles with a success rate of less than one percent are considered failures, but the matchmakers who fix them up with exactly the same batting average are considered successful. Matchmakers receive credit for successful matches without any regard for their methods or overall rate of success. Singles receive all the blame for their difficulties and none of the credit for achieving a successful relationship.

Dating is hard enough without the system being fixed against you.

Unfortunately, this is just one example of the many double standards you will face. If you become frustrated with the difficulties you are facing, married people will urge you not to give up. This is fine advice – but don't expect them to follow it as well. Many married people will try to fix you up. For one reason or another, it will not work out. They will never try to fix you up again. They will give up on helping you.

A real estate agent will not quit after showing you one property that doesn't work for you. He will use it as an opportunity to get to know your needs better and refine his selection process. There might come a point when even the best real estate agent will realize his client is not a serious buyer, or is otherwise not worth his time. Same with singles and matchmaking. Singles can be just as hard to deal with as matchmakers. But far too many people who might be able to help will feel jilted, awkward, or that they did their part after one matchmaking attempt.

I'm not suggesting they have an obligation to volunteer their time and effort, but if they really want to help, why give up so soon? Why not use this as an opportunity to fine-tune the process and do better next time? It's difficult to expect singles not to give up when those who could potentially help them give up right away. Pessimism is contagious.

Another double standard is the matter of "hunches". Married people will often use that as a basis for fixing you up with someone. They won't know you or the other person well enough to provide a meaningful basis for suggesting you meet, nor will they be interested in getting to know you better. That takes time, and why should they spend time on you? Don't they already deserve a medal of honor just for thinking of you? No matter, they have a hunch that this could work. They might have even had a hunch once before in which the two got married, so now they believe their hunches are a notch below prophecy, and you should therefore take it very seriously.

You may have already been burned many times by hunches people have had. You will learn to be leery when people approach you with hunches, and you will try to politely explain why this line does not inspire confidence in you. Married people will always dismiss your concerns. You have to give *their* hunch a chance.

You must trust their hunches, but you can never trust your own.

Yet another double standard you will face is most serious.

No matter how willing you are to step outside your comfort zone, married people will always be urging you to push the envelope further. No matter how much you are willing to change to improve your chances, it will never be enough to satisfy the critics that now you can just stay the course.

This call for flexibility doesn't go both ways. Matchmakers are notoriously rigid and defensive. A single who dares to express concern over their approach will be lucky if the matchmaker is simply offended and doesn't badmouth him to others. A baseball player with a low batting average seeks the guidance of a batting coach. A single who is encountering difficulties is expected to seek help from a "dating coach". Conversely, a matchmaker with an abysmal track record is lauded for trying and encouraged to keep making introductions. The possibility that this matchmaker has no clue and should stay far away from people's personal lives is not normally entertained.

Surely the low success rate of most matchmakers warrants an honest look in the mirror. Perhaps a complete overhaul of their methods is in order. After all, how much worse could they do if they threw singles together completely at random? (Some matchmakers, who consider age, height, and little else, essentially do that already.) Even some refinement of their methods might improve their success rate to, say, a whopping two or three percent. If nothing else, if matchmakers demonstrated the same willingness to change and improve that they demand of singles, the process would undoubtedly become more pleasant for everyone – themselves included.

Unfortunately, married people have little impetus to change their methods. Matchmakers with a poor track record continue to be in high demand. The system does not naturally weed them out as it does real estate agents, fundraisers, and headhunters with poor success rates. The only way the culture of matchmaking will change is if singles themselves insist on it. Ultimately singles are the main actors in this play – not parents, not matchmakers. You have to insist that people listen to you and take your concerns seriously, otherwise they cannot be involved in your personal life. (I am certainly not suggesting cutting off communication with one's parents, but they too need to respect certain boundaries with their adult children. In extreme cases, severely restricting the involvement of one's parents in his personal life may indeed be the healthiest option.)

Singles are afraid to speak up to matchmakers, lest they wind up with a "bad reputation". I strongly oppose this. If a matchmaker says something to you that is insulting, possibly even abusive, you owe it to yourself to protest. You do not have to sacrifice your basic dignity as a human being to get married. Here too placing one's trust in God is extremely helpful. If the matchmaker is your god, it will be that much harder to stand up for yourself. If the matchmaker is simply a possible agent of God's intervention, nothing more, then there is no reason for you to allow yourself to be mistreated. God can find another agent, and in fact He requires no agent at all.

Even if we take the religious component out of it (which, again, I do not think really can or should be done) being submissive to clueless and abusive matchmakers is not the best strategy. It is true that if you stand up to such people they will be less likely to fix you up on dates. It is also possible that they will badmouth you to other matchmakers. But do you really think people like that are your salvation as a single? Do you really want to entrust your hopes and fears to such people? If your only hope of getting married is to allow the village matchmaker to mistreat you, then I suggest you find another village.

If enough singles make it clear that they expect a certain level of respect and sensitivity, matchmakers will be forced to provide it. Whether they expect to get paid or they engage in the practice for some other motive (respect, recreation, a free pass to heaven, etc.) they need singles to play ball with them to stay in business. They need you no less than you need them – in my opinion, they need you even more. You can choose to think of yourself as a charity case or as a client. Charity cases are grateful for even a moment of attention. Clients expect professional treatment.

You are expected to treat the people you date with respect and sensitivity. You are expected to be polite and grateful to matchmakers. By all means, do so. But never forget that you have the same obligation to treat *yourself* with respect and sensitivity. This includes upholding your basic dignity when others try to make you feel small.

The overall culture of matchmaking can and should change for the better. It starts with you.

Chapter 13
Pain

Many years ago I was invited to speak before an audience of
women about issues related to dating in the Orthodox Jewish
community. This first speaker at this event was a local rabbi,
who delivered a sermon that failed to address pertinent issues,
and mainly sought to rationalize the matchmaking system as
the "traditional" way. I was extremely disappointed – I would
have preferred to meet a kindred spirit – and could hardly wait
my turn to speak. I attacked the perversion of values and lack
of intelligence that had overtaken the system, and suggested
what needed to be done. That was exactly what this audience

of mothers and grandmothers wanted to hear (which is not always the case). They had brought a lot of anger and frustration into the room, and they welcomed my blunt words.

Then came a question and answer session, but it felt more like a lynching. These ladies were not at all receptive to the other rabbi's message, and they were not shy about letting him know it. One of them would challenge something he had said, or raise an issue they felt he neglected, and he would struggle to defend himself. The moderator would then turn to me. "And what do *you* think?" she would ask, goading me to rip the man standing next to me. Much as I disagreed with his message, and much as I enjoyed having a supportive audience, part of me felt bad for him as well. He was clueless, but he was not a bad person. I was not going to publicly embarrass him. I responded honestly and to the point, without attacking him or mocking his words.

I tell this story not to portray myself as a class act (though you are welcome to draw that conclusion), but because what happened next made a very deep impression on me. The formal part of the event ended, and many of the women converged on my counterpart with more heated challenges. They wanted blood.

There was one woman, however, who stood next to the rabbi and staunchly defended him. That woman was his wife. I don't know if she actually agreed with her husband's perspective, but there was no way she was going to stand there and watch him get torn to shreds. I found it incredibly beautiful.

Being single, I was also envious. I was exhilarated with having delivered the greatest speech in history, and with receiving quite an ovation, but I was also alone. My counterpart had flopped and was rejected by the audience, but his wife was there for him. I didn't have a wife to share in my victories or support me against an angry crowd. It hurt.

There are two points I want to raise from this personal experience. Many singles, especially young singles, aspire to marry for all the wrong reasons. Their friends are getting married and they feel left behind…they feel pressure from family and their community…they need a spouse to advance in society in one way or another. This mindset is a wonderful way to mess up your life. I am all in favor of marriage, and I even believe gentle pressure can be helpful at times, but getting married for the wrong reasons is one of the worst mistakes a person can make. Communities that emphasize the wrong reasons for getting married should receive kickbacks from the divorce lawyers and courts. Those are the only people who benefit from it.

The main reason one should wish to marry is because of the first comment God makes about the human race: "It is not good for Man to be alone." There is simply no substitute for a spouse who is a true partner in life, who shares your journey with you. Friends and family are important, of course, but their fortunes are not intertwined with yours, their journey is not hand in hand with yours. A spouse is someone whose main job description is to be right there with you and for you all the way through life.

Many people will find this concept offensive simply because it is not "fair". It does not guarantee "equality of happiness" for everyone. What if someone can't find a spouse who lives up to that ideal, or anything close? What about widows and divorcees who remain alone? What if, God forbid, one's spouse becomes sick and cannot provide the support his partner needs? Am I saying that all these people cannot live an ideal life through no fault of their own?

Afraid so. Perhaps the most troubling mystery of this world is why good people often suffer so terribly. There are various responses to this, but the only one that covers all the bases is that God, as the ultimate authority, keeps certain information classified. We accept this of flawed and corrupt human governments. We should accept that God knows things that we do not and does not wish to share it with us. The person of faith believes that if he knew everything God knew, he would do things exactly the same.

Living within the context of a happy marriage is the ideal

state of human existence. Not everyone will enjoy this state of existence at all times, just as not everyone will enjoy convenience and pleasure in other aspects of life.

Some people react to this unpleasant truth by denying the truth, thereby obviating the unpleasantness. Marriage is redefined or done away with altogether in favor of "alternative" lifestyles. Marriage then becomes just another "lifestyle choice", and an inferior one at that. After all, marriage is full of obligations to another person, whereas alternative lifestyles tend to be easily disposable. Inevitably, those who seek happiness and fulfillment in other arrangements tend to resent any talk of God and His design for the human race. It's a problem if God exists, it's a bigger problem if He expresses Himself in clear terms, and it's an even bigger problem if God knows best. Best to deny any or all of the above.

This brings me to the second point. One of the most important qualities of a mature human being is the ability to deal with pain. No matter who you are, you are going to experience some sort of pain in the course of your life. The emotional pain of a single can be particularly agonizing, since it is so often unappreciated – and exacerbated – by those closest to him.

If you are going to survive as a single, you need to learn to deal with this. How you do this is something you will need to figure out in long quiet moments with yourself, and in consultation with people you trust. But you really need to do this. Many singles simply distract themselves or run away from the pain. I suggest you allow yourself to really experience it. Face it and absorb it.

The reason I suggest this is because pain, in essence, is not a bad thing. It is simply the body's way of letting you know that there is a problem, much like a car's check engine light. If you never felt pain, you would never know that you had a problem until it was too late.

The emotional pain of being single, as awful as it can be, is a reminder that you are missing something very important in your life: a partner with whom to share the journey. Your life may we wonderful in other respects – by all means, make it as wonderful as you can! – but don't allow yourself to forget that it is missing a vital component. That is the purpose of the pain. You should allow yourself to feel it at least occasionally to keep your priorities in order. Otherwise life can distract you, those hollow alternative lifestyles might seem alluring, and the possibility of your ever achieving an ideal marriage will be all but stamped out.

I cannot guarantee you will achieve it even if you do everything the right way. As I have noted many times, there is no magic formula for this, and some people will suffer for reasons that we cannot determine. Nevertheless, we have an obligation to live life the right way and strive for the right goals, even though the outcome is not in our hands.

For as long as you must remain single, be the very best single you can be. If, God forbid, your marriage is less than ideal, make the best of the situation. But don't allow pain to corrupt your thinking just to escape the pain. I say this not as a clueless preacher, but as someone who knows how bad it hurts.

Dealing with pain in a mature way will make you a better person, a stronger person, and, hopefully soon, a better spouse and parent.

As awful as pain can be, only one who has lived with it can experience true joy.

May the pain of all the good singles out there be turned to joy.

Made in United States
North Haven, CT
08 May 2024

52289459R00102